THE FOLKLORE SOCIETY

MISTLETOE SERIES

A *Collection of Highland Rites and Customes*

A COLLECTION OF HIGHLAND RITES AND CUSTOMES

COPIED BY EDWARD LHUYD FROM THE MANUSCRIPT OF THE

REV JAMES KIRKWOOD (1650-1709)

AND ANNOTATED BY HIM

WITH THE AID OF THE REV JOHN BEATON

Edited by J.L.Campbell

From MS Carte 269 in the Bodleian Library

Published by D.S.Brewer Ltd

and Rowman and Littlefield

for The Folklore Society

1975

Published by D.S.Brewer Ltd.
240 Hills Road Cambridge
and P.O.Box 24 Ipswich IP1 1JJ

ISBN O 85991 012 1 (U.K.)

First published in the U.S.A. 1975 by
Rowman and Littlefield Totowa N.J.

The Folklore Society wish to acknowledge a grant
from the Governors of Catherine McCaig's Trust
towards the cost of publication of this volume

Printed and bound in Great Britain by
Redwood Burn Limited
Trowbridge & Esher

CONTENTS

INTRODUCTION

ON 18th DECEMBER 1699 Edward Lhuyd, the great Welsh Celtic scholar and polymath, Keeper of the Ashmolean Museum at Oxford, who was then at Falkirk on his extended tour of the Celtic countries in search of linguistic, archaeological and scientific information, wrote in a letter to the Rev James Fraser, Minister of Kirkhill near Inverness[1]

'I have already about 3 sheets of the customs and Rites of the Highlands which the famous Mr Boyl[2] had procur'd from some correspondent: and would judge of the verity of these, according as we find them confirmed by your account and our own observations in the western Isles &c.'

This remark was repeated in a letter to the Rev Colin Campbell, minister of Ardchattan in Argyllshire, written by Lhuyd at Glasgow on 20th December 1699.[3] Both letters amount to questionnaires on the customs, archaeology, and language of the Highlands.

Lhuyd had been in Edinburgh during the second half of November and the first half of December 1699, having made his way there after the first part of his Highland tour in the autumn of the same year, which had taken him through Kintyre and Knapdale and Lorne to Mull and Iona.[4] On the 21st December Lhuyd was in Glasgow. That day the Rev Robert Wodrow wrote from Glasgow to Archdeacon Nicholson that 'The curiouse Mr Ed.Lhuyd has been heer this day and is gone to Ireland by the way of Kintyre'.[5] On the same page of *The Early Letters of Robert Wodrow* there follows a list headed 'Queries and things to be done in the Western Highlands'. It is clear that this list is simply a copy, or rather précis, of the same questions that Lhuyd had written to the Rev James Fraser and the Rev Colin Campbell: there are the same eight subjects for enquiry, and answers are to be left with the same person, Mr Walter Thomas at Bernard's Inn, London. The sixth subject of enquiry is:

'The peculiar games and customes observed on set dayes throughout the year, or any other fashions peculiar to the Highlanders. (Mr Edw. Lhuyd has 3 sheets of the customes and rites of the Highlands which he procured from some cor-respondent in Scotland).'

Not all the persons to whom Lhuyd appealed for help in his enquiries about the Highlands and the Highlanders were as indefatigable as Wodrow in pursuing the search for information. Wodrow did his utmost to get into touch with Lhuyd's chief informant, the Rev John Beaton, Episcopalian min-ister of Kilninian in Mull, of whom more here-after; he also wrote to John MacLean, of the Treshnish family in Mull, who was to succeed Beat-on as minister of Kilninian in 1702, on 13th April 1701, raising again the same kind of questions as Lhuyd has originally done, but under twelve head-ings.[6] The fourth of these was:

'Ane account of the fashions and customes that are peculiar to the Highlanders would be very acceptable; for their ancient bards, their peculiar games, the customes and frites [sic !] observed on set dayes throughout all the year; their mariage and funerall solemnitys, &c. I hear there was ane accompt of all thir write by some body or other to the Hble.Robert Boyl, & that there is a copy of this in some curiouse person in Mull or some of the neibouring islands his hand. I would give anything for a copy of it.'[7]

To this John MacLean replied:

'The fashions and Customes peculiar to the Highlanders, their games, and feites on set dayes, their marriage solemnities, &c., were so

2

manie, that it were tedious to make a full collection of them I know none in this countrey
[*i.e.* Mull] that hath it with him. If any has
it, I shall find it out. Mr Beaton certifies me,
that a list of all these are in the hands of Dr
Sibbald, at Edinburgh.'[8]

There can be little doubt but that 'the 3
sheets of the customes and Rites of the Highlands'
which Lhuyd said he had are the same as the 'Excerpta de libro Domini Kirkwood manuscripto dicto
A Collection of Highland Rites and Customes' contained in MS Carte 269 of the Bodleian Library,
and printed here for the first time. Sir Robert
Sibbald's address, the Bishop's Land, Edinburgh,
is entered on the first page of the MS; his name
is at the top of folio 2, verso, followed by the
words 'This Book is all in the handwriting of Ed.[d]
Lhuyd formerly Keeper of the Ashmolean Museum,
Oxford. J.P.' The last item in the MS, which apart
from Scottish, contains Cornish and Breton material, is 'A coppy of sir Robert Sibbald's paper,
directions for his honoured friend mr Lhuyd how
to trace ... the Roman wall betwixt Forth and
Clide.'[9] Sibbald (1641-1722) was the author of
Scotia Illustrata, published in 1684, a book of
great interest to Lhuyd. He was President of the
Edinburgh Royal College of Physicians and the
first Professor of Medicine at Edinburgh University.

The 'customes and Rites of the Highlands' begin
on folio 2, recto, of the MS, and are titled 'Ex
Adversarijs V.C.D.*R.S.* Excerpta de libro Domini
Kirkwood Manuscripto dicto A Collection of Highland Rites and Customes.' V.C.D. can be expanded
reasonably *Viri Clarissimi Domini* (or *Doctoris*)
and the whole translated 'From the Memoranda of
the most illustrious Sir Robert Sibbald, excerpts
from the manuscript book of the Rev Kirkwood called A Collection of Highland Rites and Customes.'[10]

Lhuyd's copy does not give any impression of being incomplete: the Rev Kirkwood's MS may well have contained other material. The *Collection* occupies folio 2, recto, to folio 26, verso, of the MS. This is exactly 48 pages, which equals the 'three sheets' mentioned by Lhuyd (one sheet = 16 pages). Lhuyd's notes on the *Collection* occupy folio 28 recto to folio 31 recto of the MS: the copy of his letter to the Rev James Fraser is between the two.

The questions relating to the *Collection of Highland Rites and Customes* are, who was the author of the original? where is the original now? how did it come into the possession, first of the Hon. Robert Boyle, and then of Sir Robert Sibbald, before being copied by Edward Lhuyd?

It has not been possible to give a certain answer to any of these questions. There is, amongst the papers of Sir Robert Sibbald in the National Library of Scotland, a MS (33.3.19) titled 'Adversaria', which contains amongst other things a copy of a letter from Lhuyd to Sibbald written at Londonderry on 20th April 1700, which is quoted here, (p.101); but there is no such item as the *Collection* in it. Nor is it in the papers of the Rev James Kirkwood in the New College Library in Edinburgh, nor in the papers of the Rev Robert Kirk, who as we shall see may well have been connected with it, in Edinburgh University Library. However it is possible to make some reasonable surmises about these things. The Hon. Robert Boyle, the famous chemist and natural philosopher, who was born on 25th January 1627, was living in London in the 1680s. One of his many worthy interests was the promotion of the Protestant Irish Gaelic version of the Bible. His attention was drawn to the fact that 'Irish' was also spoken over a wide area of Scotland, and he was persuaded to extend his charitable efforts in that direction. In the cause of promoting the circulation of the Gaelic Bible in the Highlands, he had the particular assistance of two Scottish Episcopalian ministers, the Rev Robert Kirk, minister of Aberfoyle, best known as the author of the *Secret Commonwealth*, a famous account of Highland beliefs in elves, fairies, and second sight, who came to London in September 1689 to see the edition of the Irish Bible printed in Roman characters through the press, and the Rev James Kirkwood, a native of Dunbar, then parson of Astwick in Bedfordshire. Kirk and Kirkwood were personal friends; Kirkwood also knew Boyle personally and had a high regard for him. Five of Kirkwood's letters to Boyle, written between 5th November 1687 and 30th October 1690, are printed in Thomas Birch's *Life of the Honourable Robert Boyle* (London, 1744).

These are all on the subject of the provision of the Irish Bible for the Scottish Highlanders. Kirkwood wrote also a letter to Dr Wotton on 22nd June 1702 giving a general account of the matter, in which he remarked of Boyle that 'I reckon it one of the blessings of my life, to have been acquainted with so extraordinary a person, whose company I always found very delightful and edifying.'[11]

It would therefore not be surprising if Boyle, himself a seventh son and born in Ireland, had expressed an interest in the customs of the Highlanders whom he hoped the circulation of the Irish Bible would help to redeem from 'barbarity', and had asked either the Rev James Kirkwood or the Rev Robert Kirk to write an account of them. The possibility that Kirk was the original author of most of the *Collection* cannot be ignored, following the publication by Professor Mario Rossi of the fuller version of Kirk's *Secret Commonwealth of Elves Fauns and Fairies* from MS La.III 551 of Edinburgh University in the *Storia e Pensiero* series under the title *Il Cappellano delle Fate* at Naples in 1964, preceded by his article 'Text-Criticism of Robert Kirk's *Secret Commonwealth*' in

5

the Edinburgh Bibliographical Society's *Transactions* ten years earlier. On p.259 of Vol.III of
the latter Professor Rossi printed an alternative,
and presumably original, title of the *Secret
Commonwealth* from this MS, of which the conclud-
ing words, deleted in the MS, are:

'With ane accompt of the Irish-Charmes being
part of a larger discourse, of the Ancient customes of the Scotish-Irish, their nature, habit,
manner of warr, husbandry, the air & product-
iones of their Countrey &c.'

The 'Irish-Charmes' were included in the MS
La.III 551 version of the Secret Commonwealth: the
account of the 'Ancient customes of the Scotish-
Irish' is exactly what we have in the *Collection*
copied by Edward Lhuyd from Kirkwood's MS in the
possession of Sir Robert Sibbald, with the ex-
ception of parts of sections 2 and 3, and the
last section, which describes curiosities in Mid
and East Lothian and the Merse, Kirkwood's native
district, and has nothing to do with the Highlands. Moreover there is a marked similarity between certain passages in the *Collection* and in
the *Secret Commonwealth*, see the notes to Section
7 here. Professor Rossi shows that a motive of
Kirk's in writing the Secret Commonwealth was the
entertainment or instruction of Lady Stillingfleet, whose husband had recently become Bishop
of Worcester: Dr Thomas Dent, prebendary of West-
minster, is quoted in Thomas Birch's *Life of the
Honourable Robert Boyle* as saying that Boyle had
'always the greatest value and esteem' for Bishop
Stillingfleet's 'depth of learning and solid
judgment'.

Boyle died on 31st December 1691, the same year
that Lhuyd was appointed Keeper of the Ashmolean
Museum at Oxford. Lhuyd did not begin his great
tour of the Celtic countries until the spring of
1697, and it seems unlikely that he ever received

the MS of the *Collection* from Boyle directly. In any case what we have in MS Carte 269 is a copy of it in Lhuyd's own handwriting. It is clear, as one approaches the end of the copy, that it was made in something of a hurry; and it is also clear that Lhuyd was puzzled by some of the Scots words occurring in the *Collection*, and also sometimes had difficulties in reading the original handwriting.

It is curious that Lhuyd made no allusion to the authorship of the *Collection* in his letters to the Rev James Fraser and the Rev Colin Campbell, nor in his talk with Robert Wodrow. Lhuyd was certainly in possession of the copy he had made of the *Collection* when he reached Coleraine in the north of Ireland in February 1700, for it was there that he met the Rev John Beaton, Episcopalian minister of Kilninian in Mull, who gave him much interesting information about old Gaelic MSS in his possession, and about Gaelic folklore,[12] and whose comments on various points in the *Collection* Lhuyd noted carefully. Being the last learned member of the famous Beaton family, formerly hereditary physicians to the Lords of the Isles, and owning a large number of their Gaelic MSS, John Beaton had a profound knowledge of the traditions and folklore of his fellow Gaels, and the information he gave to Lhuyd in commenting on the *Collection*, and otherwise, is of great value. He was certainly responsible for most, and possibly for all, of the additional material Lhuyd added to his copy of the *Collection*, and it is likely to have been his pronunciation that Lhuyd took down in Welsh spelling when recording Gaelic words. Beaton was also probably responsible for a number of deletions of misleading statements, see e.g. the Section 30, 'Anent Thunder'. Thus annotated, Lhuyd's copy of the MS is considerably more interesting than the original MS of the *Collection* would have been.

In preparing the *Collection of Highland Rites and Customes* for publication, I have divided Lhuyd's notes at the end of the MS and placed them after the sections of the *Collection* to which they refer. I have then added my own notes, which consist for the most part of references to seventeenth and eighteenth century writers like Kirk, Martin, Burt, Pennant, Ramsay of Ochtertyre, and E.D.Clarke where these confirm or illuminate statements made in the *Collection*. I have also given many references to the books by J.Gregorson Campbell on *Witchcraft and Second Sight*, and on *Superstitions of the Scottish Highlands*, which, although published considerably later, illustrate in a remarkable way the persistence of the Gaelic oral tradition in a remote Hebridean island (Tiree). The manuscript collections of Fr Allan McDonald, made in Eriskay and South Uist between 1887 and 1905, contain much the same kind of material.

In editing the text I have preserved Lhuyd's asterisks, which were apparently intended to mark certain words or passages that interested him particularly. I have printed what are obviously additions to the text, probably most of them comments by the Rev John Beaton, in italics. Passages deleted in the MS are placed between daggers. My own additions to the text, including the normal forms of Gaelic words occurring in it, are placed in square brackets. I have expanded Lhuyd's 'yͤ' 'yͭ' and '&' regularly into 'the' 'that' and 'and' Numerals are sometimes written in full.

I have added an appendix of Notes on *Edward Lhuyd in the Scottish Highlands*, most of which have to do with the Rev John Beaton himself or with folklore information which he gave to Lhuyd, as this is relevant to the present publication. I have also added a Glossarial Index of Gaelic and Scots words that occur in the *Collection*.

In conclusion, I wish to express my sincere

8

thanks to the persons who have encouraged this
work, or assisted my enquiries, particularly
Professor I.Ll.Foster, óf Oxford University;
Messrs D.M.Lloyd and I.C.Cunningham of the National Library of Scotland; D.Murison of the Scottish
National Dictionary; C.P.Finlayson of Edinburgh
University Library; J.Howard of the New College
Library, Edinburgh; L.P.Townsend, Archivist of the
Royal Society; W.O'Sullivan, Trinity College, Dublin; and the Librarian of the London Library. I am
also much obliged to the authorities of the Bodleian Library for allowing me to have photocopies
of this part of MS Carte 269, and for permission
to publish the *Collection of Highland Rites and
Customes*; and to Signora Elisa Rossi for permission to quote from the late Dr Mario Rossi's
Il Cappellano delle Fate.

J.L.CAMPBELL

Isle of Canna

9

NOTES TO THE INTRODUCTION

1. Lhuyd's copy of this letter is in Bodleian MS Carte 269 folios 26-28. It is printed here, p.11. The Rev James Fraser was the author of the Wardlaw MS printed by the Scottish History Society, first series No.47 (1905), "Chronicles of the Frasers", edited by William MacKay. He was minister of Kirkhill from 1662 to 1709. If he answered Lhuyd's letter, his reply has been lost.

2. The Hon.Robert Boyle (1627-1691) the natural philosopher and chemist, who took a leading part in the foundation of the Royal Society.

3. Printed in ELSH p.4-5. The original is in Edinburgh University Library. The Rev Colin Campbell was a mathematician and a correspondent of Isaac Newton's.

4. See ELSH xvi-xxi; TELI 222.

5. *Early Letters of Robert Wodrow*, edited by L.W. Sharp, p.32. Scottish History Society, Third Series XXIV, 1937.

6. *ibidem* pp.159-162.

7. *ibidem*, 160.

8. Quoted from *Analecta Scotica* in ELSH, p.31.

9. Catalogue of Carte Papers, p.154.

10. I am obliged to Mr D.M.Lloyd of the National Library of Scotland for this suggestion.

11. *Op. cit.* 397.

12. See ELSH pp.12-87, and the Appendix here.

PART OF THE LETTER [FROM EDWARD LHUYD] TO THE
REVD Mr JAMES FRASER MINISTER OF KIRKHILL IN THE
AIRD NEAR INVERNES:

Dated at Falkirk in Sterlingshire Dec.18 1699.

... But it lies not in their way to be so immed-
iately assisting in the undertaking I am engaged
in; in regard, they are strangers to the old Scottish Language and customes, the comparing of which
with the Welsh, Cornish and Armorican is one part
of my design. I therefore make bold to addresse
myself to you for your kind assistance; and in-
treat you that besides your own trouble, you would
prevail with some friend or two (in regard it may
prove tedious) to contribute their helping hand.
In return I can only promise that if hereafter it
may lye in my way to be serviceable to your self
or any friend, in my station at Oxford, I shall
very faithfully observe your directions, and if I
shall understand that any new book there may be
acceptable to you, I shall study to expresse my
Gratitude. Now the Requests I have chiefly to make
(so far as they occur to my thoughts at present)
are as follows.

1. An interpretation of the Nouns in Mr Ray's
Dictionariolum Trilingue; with the Addition of
the Verbs and Adjectives in the vulgar Nomencla-
ture into the Northern Ersh would be very acceptable.

2. A catalogue of the towns, castles, villages,
mountains, vales, lochs and rivers, within ten
(or twenty) miles; with an interpretation of such
of these names as are indubitably intelligible;
and queries or conjectures about some of the
others.

3. Some acc^t of the Barrows or artificial mounts;
of monumental stones, whether those inscrib'd
with Letters, or other carving; or those plac'd

in a circular order, or vast stones placed on the tops of others pitch'd in the ground.

4. An acc^t of the Amulets and charms &c. viz. Adderstones, Toadstones, Cock-knee-stones, snail-stones, mole-stones, Leag, Elf Arrows and the like; with any other *Relations* that may fall under this Head. And as many of those curiosities as may be procur'd without much expence are earn-estly desir'd.

5. Any Coin, Fibula, or other old brasse unten-sil; or small stones of any peculiar figure (whether natural or artificial) would be no lesse acceptable.

6. The peculiar Games and customes observ'd on set days throughout the year; and any other fash-ions that you know peculiar to the Highlands. I have already ab^t 3 sheets of the customes and Rites of the Highlands; which the famous Mr Boyl had procur'd from some correspondent: and would judge of the verity of these according as we find them confirm'd by your acc^t and our own observa-tions in the Western Isles, &c.

7. A catalogue of the Highland Poets of note, and of all the other writers on what subject soever in the Ersh or Scottish Irish. When they flour-ish'd: what they writ: how large their works; with the three or four initial and final words; and where their works may be seen at present.

8. A catalogue of the Christian names purely Ersh; with a mark of distinction to those still in use.

Thus sir, you find I have cutt out for your self and your friends a great deal of work, but I pretend not to be your Taskmaster. An answer to any of these Heads would be very thankfully re-ceiv'd. And for the time; about May next will be very seasonable and a twelvemonth hence not too late.

Pray pardon this trouble given you by (worthy S^r) your very humble serv^t E.L.

Any papers, &c. will come safe to my hands, if directed to be left either with Mr James Paterson at the Taylor's Land in the Cow-gate, Edenbrough or with Mr Walter Thomas at Bernards Inne, London.

A COLLECTION OF HIGHLAND RITES AND CUS-TOMES

1. OBSERVATIONS UPON THEIR COMPUTATION OF TYME
2. THEIR LANGUAGE
3. THEIR HABIT AND ORNAMENTS
4. BUILDING
5. THEIR BEDDING AND SLEEPING
6. THEIR CLANNES AND NAMES
7. THEIR MEAT AND THEIR DRINK
8. OF THEIR AUGURY, PREDICTIONS, AND SECOND SIGHT
9. THEIR BARDS
10. THEIR WARRS AND ARMOUR
11. THEIR FEUDS
12. THEIR FLITTING
13. THEIR HOSPITALITY
14. THEIR MONUMENTS
15. MUSIC
16. THEIR FEASTS
17. THEIR FARMERS
18. THEIR TRYING OFFENCES
19. PLOUGHING, HARROWING, DUNGING THE GROUND
20. CLER SHEANCHAIN
21. THEIR DEFERENCE AND REGARD TO SOME PERSONS
22. THEIR FUEL
23. FIRE AND SALT
24. THEIR HUNTING
25. BUYING AND SELLING
26. FISHING AND SHIPPING
27. CHARMES
28. DISEASES AND PHYSIC
29. MUSIC (*deleted, already described in section 15*)
30. ANENT THUNDER
31. CALLING PERSONS BY THEIR NAMES
32. THIGGING
33. BIRTH AND BAPTISM
34. FOSTERING
35. DREAMS
36. LAKEWAKES
37. BURIAL

Ex Adversarijs V.C.D.R.S.
Excerpta de libro Domini Kirkwood
Manuscripto dicto *A Collection of
Highland Rites & Customes.*

1. OBSERVATIONS UPON THEIR COMPUTATION OF TYME

They borrow the names of Feasts moveable and im-
movable from the Christian Account; onely they
have mercat days held in Saints names unknown in
other Languages as *Feil Seirbh* (thought to be St.
Serf or Serbanus) *Feil Domhiṅg̣aṛt, makessag, haden,
moden* &c.

They reckon not by moneths of 30 or 31 days but
by four weeks computing by the Moon, wch. they
much observe almost in all maters.

They have no proper names to any month, except
April which they call *Diblin*; onely, they reckon
them by certain Seasons as the most cold Season
fourteen days before Candlmasse and 14 days after
they term by an irony *Faoldach* [Faoilteach] the
loving Season. The 8 days after that, they call
Feadag id est the whistling week of cold winds.
8 days after that *Gear[r]shion .i.* curt, incon-
stant tempests. Fourteen days before *Beltan* [Be-
alltainn] or May and fourteen days after they call
Ceothom i.e. the soft misty moneth: fourteen days
before Lammas [,] *Eochar* [Iuchar] *.i.* the Key of
Harvest. [+]They have an other Key called *Feil
Hethan* [*Féill Sheathain*] thereafter[+]. *Feil Eoin
i.e. St John's.*

The Number <u>Three</u> is sacred with them (hence in
any hard work we say thrice of all things) next to
that Nine. When anything succeeds not for three
times they try it nine times and then give it over
ordinarily. *This from the Trinity says Mr Beaton.
They honour also the number seven.* [Illegible] *the
seven angels.*

17

*January is call'd *mîos marbh* [the dead month]
wch is divided in *Fwylliach gabhri* [*Faoilleach
geamhraidh*] i.e. *Fwyliach* hyemalis and *Fwyll*
[blank in MS].*

Fwylliach gavri [the Faoilleach of winter] is
the last 15 days of January. And the first 15 days
of February is called *Fùilliach errich* [*Faoilleach
earraich*] i.e. the Fuilliach of the Spring. Both
these computed together makes the *mios marbh*.

Kalwyn or *Kolwyn* [*Calluinn, Colluinn*] is the
last night of the old year, and that night they go
about seeking bread and cheese. This cheese they
keep til that night 12 month; and if they are be-
clouded at any time either on sea or mountain,
they bruise a litle of it and through [*sic*] it
into the aer to dispel the Clouds; or mist. Prob.
est.

Mios y Fylih [*mîos an Fhaoillich*] is ye winter
and spring season above mentioned. *Kyikiys garrain*
[*Cóicthigheas gearrain*] alias *garrain borb* [*Gearran borb*, wild Gearran] i.e. *iumentum audax* [an
audacious beast of burden].

Seachdown no Kehar la Feddag [*Seachdmhain nan
Ceithir là Feadaig*] i.e. the Plover week.

(Folio 29) The first three days of March *Eym
scobyg na Faoilach* [*Amm sgobadh nam Faoilleach,*
the biting time of the Faoilleachs] because it's
a severe tyme then with the Catle.

The last 15 days of April and the first 15 of
May are call'd *Keitan* [*Céitein*] viz. the 15 of
April *Keitan aerrich* [*Céitein earraich*, the
Céitein of spring] and the other *Keitan savrih*
[*Céitein Samhraidh*, the Céitein of summer].

Shrove Tuesday is call'd *Mart-inid*: and Ash
Wednesday *Kedin yn lẁairih* [*Ceudaoin an luaith-
ridh*]. *Donach na Slat* [*Dòmhnach nan Slat*] Palm
Sunday. *Donach Kask* [*Dòmhnach Càsg'*] Easter Sun-

day: the thirsday before *Dierdŵyn Martain* [*Diard-
aoin Màrtain*, St Martin's Thursday]; because then
they barberize and not before during Lent.
   La baltin [*Là Bealltainn*] May day. *Baltin vôr*
[*Bealltainn mhór*] the 1st of May and *Baltin beag*
[*Bealltainn bheag*] that day 8 days.
   Lwnystal [*Lùnasdal*] is Lambmasse; *Feil Cholym
Kil* [*Féill Cholum Cille*] Kolumb Kil's [St
Columba's] Feast [June 9th.] *Feil na Krohi* [*Féill
na Croiche*] Festum crucis [presumably the Feast of
the Exaltation of the Cross, September 14th.]
   Koila deag na Davair [*Cói' là deug na Dàmhair*]
the Fortnight of Rutting (in October). Because
'tis rutting time with the deer. The great stags
*sydh yn ymrain y pryd ymma mewn cors. herwydh idho
ev bhrydhwydio am ewig wen a chyshæ cochion ag
etto medhy i chael hi* [which are rutting at this
time in a bog because of their desire for a white
hind with red legs and still failing to get her].
   Mem. to enq. about the ceremony of St Bride on
the 1st of February.

Editor's Notes

St Serf or Servanus was associated with Culross in
Fife; possibly lived in the sixth century. His day
was July 1st. See A.O.A. I 127-130; Skene, II 31,
255-258.

Domhnigart: the italics indicate that Lhuyd was
not sure of the reading. Eight persons named Dom-
angart are mentioned by A.O.A.; the only one connected with the Church was lector of Turriff in
1131-2, see A.O.A. II 178. Is it possible that the
original writer of the MS confused the names Dom-
angart and Donnan, the latter the saint, well
known in the Highlands, who was martyred on the
Isle of Eigg in 617?

Makessag: St Kessock was associated with the Loch
Lomond district. He lived in the sixth century,
and was the national patron of Scotland before St
Andrew. His day was March 10 (old style), 22nd
(new style). See J.G.C.(W) 259, who says that his
fair was called *Féill mo Cheasaig* in Gaelic.

Haden presumably = St Aidan of Lindisfarne, d. 651,
who went from Iona to be the apostle of Northum-
bria. His day is August 31st.

Moden: St Moden was a sixth century abbot, who
preached in the district of the Forth, especially
at Falkirk (*Eaglais Bhreac* in Gaelic). He was patron of the High Church at Stirling. His day is
February 4th. See Skene II 282.

Beltan: See Martin 105; Pennant I 111; R.O. II
439-445; J.G.C.(W) 267-272.

Lammas, August 1st, old style, 12th new style. See
J.G.C.(W) 277-8.

Feil Hethan = Féill Sheathain, 24th June/6th July,
see J.G.C.(W) 276.

Eochar, see J.G.C.(W) 279.

three times: *times* replaces *things* in the MS.

For the Highlanders' regard for the numbers three
and nine, see e.g. Martin 113; R.O. II 452; D.McPh.
196.

On days of the year generally, see R.O. 436-448;
John MacKay, *Aimsirean na Bliadhna,* in *Guth na
Bliadhna* V 340-361 and VI 76-104, and *Notes on the
Gaelic Calendar*, by 'Fionn', *ibidem*, V 187-196 and
285-297.

the ceremony of St Bride, see Martin 119; R.O. II
447; GWSU 2nd ed. under LEABADH BHRIGHIDE pp. 159
and 311.

2. THEIR LANGUAGE

Of their Language there are several dialects, which make them to one another partly unintelligible, partly ridiculous. The purest dialect is thought to be in Cantyre, Argyle and the Western Isles. Where they confine with the Lowlands they speak most corrupt. They can discern the countrey one is of by his dialect.

Their language is both copious and significant. The new Testament is translated it in an [sic] Irish print, the psalms lately by Mr Kirk in an ordinary character. The old Testament was translated by Bishop Bedel and is lately printed in the Saxon character. Knoxes's Liturgy too, is translated into it. Their Language is Near akin to the Latin and next to the French; some what also to the Hebrew and Greek.

They pronounce as the French write, They abound with Proverbs. In the South every Countrey has its own accent and mode of Speech; by which ordinarly they know one an other.

*In Teviot dale for *all* they say *aw*: for Andrew David* for *Robert Habb*: for *eleven*, *leen*: for seaven, seen; A Bair they call Bread: When they are surpriz'd at anything they say Bennadistie i.e. Benedicite, for Craig, Craag: for away, awaas; for me, mey; Be, Bey, etc.

Lhuyd's Notes (Folio 29)

Every Shire in Scotland has a different Dialect, but that of Mull is esteem'd the purest Irish next unto that of Connacht Irish in Ireland.

Editor's Notes

The argument about where the 'best Gaelic' is spoken still goes on today. Lhuyd's note shows

21

that the Rev John Beaton had spoken up for Mull.

The asterisks in the last paragraph are Lhuyd's.

David is probably a copying mistake of Lhuyd's for *Dand*, the Scots pet name for Andrew. *Habb* likewise is presumably a copying mistake for *Rabb*.

A bair they call Bread is probably a copying mistake for something like *A bair bannock they call bread*. Bair = bere or four-rowed barley. I am obliged to Dr David Murison for this suggestion.

3. THEIR HABIT AND ORNAMENTS

They alter not much their Habit; except in the
fashion of their sleevs. Their ordinary habit at
home is their Trewes and when they goe abroad they
use belted playd; and short hose.

The woemans playd is belted also and sides to
the ground. They wear a Broach on the Breast of
Silver or Brasse according to their Quality. The
poorer women wear nothing but their plaid.

Their plaids serve them for Bed-covering,
Bodily cloathing; Towel, Sayls, Mortclaith etc.

Women of Better Quality wear broad leather
Belts with studs of Silver or Brasse.

All the common people wear Rings on their
Fingers; some of Horn, some of Brasse, some of
Silver, &c. *This is in the mainland not much in
the Isles.*

In the South the women have fine plaiding
blankets which they wear instead of plaids.

The men at the Head of the waters in Teviotdale
and Forest wear black coats and elswhere they use
blew coats.

They use to put on the right foot hose and the
Right foot shoe first.

Lhuyd's Notes (Folio 29)

The milkwomen use brasse rings and sometimes
milk through them against witchcraft; viz. against
that the wiches may never milk their cows.

In the making their broags and hose; they make
a distinction between their right and left. At the
lanshing out of a boat, they cry out to use their
right hand.

Editor's Notes

For descriptions of the dress of the Highland-

23

ers, see Burt, II 84-105; Martin, 206-9; Pennant
I 210, 213. There are many allusions to it in
seventeenth century waulking songs, see e.g. FFSU
and HF.

The woemans playd is belted: The asterisks are
Lhuyd's.

4. BUILDING

When they buyld a new house, the 1st fire they kindle they hide iron uder the Hearth.

They cast also a Goats head over the couples, which if it meet with no stop, they think a good omen.

At the setting up of the couples a woman is necessary to put to her hand.

Their houses for the most Sheilds made of earth or stone and clay and riveted with Rivets. In Loch Aber the Walls of their houses is of Juniper and such like pletted together.

The Chimney in the midle of the House, to which the vent answers. The Company sits round about the Ground [blank in MS] it burns. In the South the old houses are T'eel houses for defence against sudden risings. Of these there are in Redward Forrest about 54.

Editor's Notes

For descriptions of the houses of the Highlanders, see e.g. Burt I 110-112; Pennant I 132, II 262, 318.

Sheilds = huts or cottages (*sheals*).

Rivets here could only mean *clenched nails*; but it seems more likely that there has been a copying mistake and that the original word was Scots *divots* sods of turf.

upon the Ground: There is a blank space in the MS after *Ground*. Possibly *where* can be supplied.

T'eel, underdotted by Lhuyd to imply doubt, must be a copying mistake for *peel*. The *peel house* is the standard square keep of the borders.

5. THEIR BEDDING AND SLEEPING

They ly on the Ground either on Straw, Hay, Fairns, or Feathers according to the Season of the year. Their Bed-cloathes are ordinarily of marld [spring] plaids some are very fine and they make Propines of them. Except among the Gentry there are no sheets.

The common Servants lye promiscuously head and throwes.

If any wake out of their sleep suddenly by a Fearfull Dream; they say it is for want of Saining or praying ere they went to bed.

When they go to bed, they crosse themselvs and say the Lords Prayer, They'l not sleep on a Fayry hill. They roll up themselves in the bedpleds.

In some of the Isles they make use of Quairrs* to conciliat rest and sleep.

They'l not rise out of bed both at once.

Editor's Notes

For descriptions of the bedding of the High-landers, see Martin 196; Burt I 111.

Marld = variegated. Lhuyd has underdotted this, and has added *spring* above, perhaps from a Scots informant (*spraing*, a long stripe of varigated streak).

Propines = presents, gifts.

head and Throwes = head to feet alternatively.

Saining = crossing themselves, making the sign of the Cross.

Quairrs = ? The asterisk is Lhuyd's.

6. THEIR CLANNES AND NAMES

Clan in the Irish signifies Children. The most
numerous is the *Clan O dwin* [Clann O Duibhne] .i.
Campbells so called from the first man of that
name who was O dwin.

Next are the MacDonalds of which are several
Subalternal Clans, as Mac Alestr, MacLain, Macjons,
MacNabs, Mac Clauds, Gordons, MacEnzies, Mackin-
Tosh, Frazers, Camerons, MacAnalds, MacNeils, Mac-
Lachlands, Lamonds, Chattans, Buchannans, MacDug-
als. B. *These formerly held of the McDonalds*.

They are able to reckon their Genealogy for 20
degrees.

Their Tribes have generally peculiar names as
the MacLains have Hector, Allen, & Lachland: The
Frazers Ferquard, The MacDugals Dugal.

They design the Chief of the Family from the
first Founder therof.

For Distinction among their names, they call a
person by five or seaven names viz. Ieam Mac Owle
&c. reckoning Father, Grandfather, Great Grandfather &c. by their Christen'd names in a long web.

In the South the Great Clans are Humes, in the Merce.

In Teviot Dale Scots, Kers.

Liddisdale Eliots Armstrong:

Anandale Johnsons,

Nithisdale Maxwells

Chadisdale Hamiltons

Carrik Kenedy.

Kile Boyd

Cuninghame Wallace Crawford,

Galloway; Gordon, Stuart, Mac-culloch, MacDugal,
        Agnew.

Cathnesse, Sinclare.

Lennox, Flemming, Colyhoon.

Rosse, Rosse, MacEnzi.

Stirlingshire; Stirlin, Levistone.

Fife; Weems, Aston, Betoun, Halket.

Anguse: Lyon, Carnagie

Perthshire. Drummond, Murray.
Merns, Arbuthnet, Burnet, Straitton, Falkner,
    Ogilby.
Aberdennshire; Skeen, Meingnies *vulgo Minies*,
    Hay, Keith.
Murray Dumbar, Brodie.

Lhuyd's Notes (Folio 30)

The MacDonalds says Mr Beaton are incomparably the most numerous, and take precedence.

Editor's Notes

O dwin. Lhuyd wrote *Odwin*, but the name of course in Gaelic is O Duine or O Duibhne. Diarmaid O Duibhne, one of the Fingalian heroes, was the eponymous ancestor of the Campbells. See the MS History of Craignish, S.H.S. Miscellany IV 194.

several Subalternal Clans: most of the clans mentioned were feudatories at one time or another of the MacDonalds as Lords of the Isles.

MacLains and *MacClauds* were crossed off this list each with two crosses, in the MS. This may have been under the Rev John Beaton's influence: Beaton was a supporter of the MacLeans, and both the MacLeans and the MacLeods had had bitter feuds with the MacDonalds in the second half of the sixteenth century, after the Lordship of the Isles had broken down. *MacClauds* so spelt possibly because the name of their supposed ancestor (Leod) was formerly Latinized as *Claudius*.

MacAnalds may be a copying mistake for *MacRonalds*.

20 degrees. Alexander Campbell the writer of the MS History of Craignish remarked that 'no people have their History so exactly keept by Tradition as the Highlanders.' S.H.S. Misc, IV 193.

28

Ieam mac Owle: Ieam in the MS could be read as *Geam*, the word is presumably a copying mistake for *Iain*. The full name would be *Iain mac Dhubhghaill* in conventional spelling, = John son of Dugal. On Highland names, see Burt II 17-20.

vulgo Minies was written by Lhuyd above *Meingnies*.

7. THEIR MEAT AND THEIR DRINK

In the time of scarcity they launce their cows neck and make meat of their Blood; *with butter or milk when boyld in time of Dearth.*

The Lochabermen when they Kil a Cow, hang up the whole carcase, and eat it as they need. *This is all over the Highlands.* When they are in the Hills they boyl their Flesh in the Belly or Haggas with a fire of the bones *and other fuel.* They boyl also the Flesh in a Haggis. They live most on milk and Fishes. They (in the Isles especially) have a way of drying their corn before it be threshen; by burning the straw and it together, keeping the corn very dextrously from being wrongd with the Fire; then they grind it in Querns, *This expeditious way of drying corn is frequently used in Kery, Ireland.*

The Gentleman's Bread is made like a Triangle: The commons of a round Form.

The bake every day, morning and evening, not excepting the Lords day.

They have no ovens nor chimneys.

Except that they may eat a litle in the morning, usually they eat none til night, when they come in from their labour.

In great Houses when they kil Kine, in some places every Servant has his own piece assign'd v.g. the Smith, the Head; the Piper the Liver; they who sing best the rump &c.

The Master gets onely the four Quarters.

When they are at dinner they lay a white rod acrosse the door, and none who see it will come in. This they doe also when they are on servets. When they kill a Calf, they must not speak a word til the head be taken off; otherwise they are punished.

Their Drink is meal and Water boyld together, called <u>Brochan</u>. Of Aqua Vitæ they drink plentifully; some will drink a Mutchkin of it <u>at a</u>

Draught, espec. in Summer.

*Generally Masters and Servants diet together.
'Tis commonly contrary, M.ͬ *Beaton.*

They'l not eat the first bread of a Crop without Butter.

In time of their Diet there are some they call Hallinshakers who look gaping over a partition waiting for some Vicutals.

They have a tall-man who attends them at meat called *Sleokach an lâr* or *Lekach lâr [eachlach ùrlair]*. They usually eat but twise a day; their Breakfast called *Diot lâ* and supper *Cuid-oidh [Cuid-oidhche]*. Of old all sat together; and what was broken above the salt-fat was sent down the Board.

When good eaters continue lean they say, they are attended with one *Ceart Chomach* who takes away the Foyson of his meat betwixt his hand and his Mouth; the *Caninus Appetitus* they call *Lon Krŷish [Lòn-chraois]* as if it were a Gnawing meagr; insatiable creature, within them.

They say the Elfs feed on the faison of our corn whereof they make an Excellent Liquor. Others of grosser Bodies are heard to take Bread.

Instead of Salt to their cheese they use Seaware (wrack) which they burn; and with the Ashes therof they salt their cheese, by rubbing it outwardly; after some days they wash it.

Theyl not make any butter on Fryday.

For salt to their butter in some places they cut Sea Dulse very small and mix it therwith. *This is true but not usd as salt.*

Editor's Notes

For the Highlanders' practice of bleeding their cattle when food was scarce in time of spring, see Burt II 28; Pennant II 387.

meat is substituted for *bread* deleted.

Belly or Haggas is substituted for *skin* in the MS. But both were used. Bishop Leslie (1578) wrote that 'Gif necessitie vrge, this day they take the hail meklewame (= whole stomach) of ane slain ox, they turn and dicht (= prepare) it, they fill it partlie with watir partlie with flesche, they hing it in the cruik or a sting (= pole), eftir the maner of a pott, and sa thay kuik it verie commodiouslie upon the fyre'. George Buchanan (1582) wrote in his Latin history of Scotland that 'they boil the flesh with water poured into the paunch or the skin of the animal they kill ... they drink the juice of the boiled flesh'. (H.B. 164, 233). See also Burt II 173.

by burning the straw: this was called graddaning. See Martin, 204; Lhuyd, *Archaeologia Britannica* 430, under *graddan*; Boswell, 134; Pennant II 322-3.

servets = serviettes, salvers.

the Smith, the head cp. Martin 109.

a white rod acrosse the door cp. Martin 107. In 1595 Margaret Campbell, widow of John Oig Campbell of Cabrachan, in her confession regarding the murder of the Laird of Calder, told how when the conspirators met at Dunollie, 'MacCouil [MacDougall of Dunollie] put the sloit on the dur and John [Campbell of] Auchavulling without the dor with ane quhyte battoune in his hand to keep all folks frae us'. (S.H.S., *Highland Papers* I 164).

Brochan: see Martin 76, 201, 233; Pennant II 358.

a mutchkin: about three quarters of a pint.

Hallinshakers = beggars.

tall-man: no such term is to be found in the O.E.D. or the S.N.D. But there is a Scots word *toilman* = toiler which would fit the context here.

Sleokaçh (? *Sleakach*) *an lâr* or *Lekach lâr*. The
last three words were added by Lhuyd. It seems to
me that this can only stand for *eachlach-ùrlair* in
its original sense of 'household messenger', see
T.F.O'Rahilly, Miscellanea, *Erıú* IX 15, on this
term.

eat but twise a day: cp. George Buchanan, H.B.
234; Martin, 201.

fat = vat.

foyson = essence, nutriment

chomach substituted for *chonnach*, deleted.

This and the following paragraph would be more
appropriate in the next section. They recall very
strongly a similar passage in Kirk's *Secret Commonwealth*

> 'They avouch that a Heluo, or Great Eater,
> hath a voracious Elve to be his attender called
> *geirt coimitheth* a joint-eater or just-halver,
> feeding on the pith and quintessence of what the
> man eats, and that therefore he continues lean
> like a hauke or heron, notwithstanding his de-
> vouring appetite'.

(MS La III 551, see ICDF 224-226). In MS 308, as
quoted by ICDF, the Gaelic words are *cert-coim'
itech*; in MS 5022, the source of Andrew Lang's edition, they are omitted. They seem to stand for
ceart-choimh-ithiche, 'just co-eater'.

Caninus appetitus 'the greedy-worm, when one eats
much' (Ainsworth's Latin Dictionary, London, 1736).
Dwelly gives 'canine appetite' as one of the mean-
ings of *lòn-chraois*, without any explanation.

elfs feed on the faison of our corn: cp. Kirk 67,
ICDF 214, 'others (i.e. other fairies) feed more
gross on the foyson or substance of Corns and
Liquors ... in this same Age, they are at times

heard to bake bread'. This suggests strongly that
Lhuyd's 'take Bread' is a copying error for 'bake
Bread'.

instead of salt in their cheese: Martin tells how
the burnt ashes of seaweeds were used to preserve
cheese, instead of salt (p.186). In his book on
St Kilda he says (p. 114) that only the shortest
seaweed that grows on the rocks was used for this
purpose.

8. OF THEIR AUGURY, PREDICTIONS AND SECOND SIGHT

*When they hear first the G̣o̧ṵg̣o̧ṵṣ (Cookoe) they observe
whether they are then fasting, or not: if fasting
they take it as an ill omen. They observe also to
what Airth they are looking; and accordingly they
conclude they are to live in that same Airth that
year. Thus the Observants observe. Also they look
to the Sole of their left foot, and if they get
ane black hair its an ill omen; if white good; if
mixt indiffrent.

When they are in the fields at meat if a Corby
come near they throw it meat, which if it take
they think that they shall live that year, otherwise they expect death. If they see a Snayl in a
base place, they think it an ill sign.

If Bees live long they think the master a good
man.

In the South they are great noticers of the
Pyŏts crying about the Houses of sick Folk as a
Token of Death and of Ravens. Sometimes they call
the piots foretokeners of Strangers.

*When they hear the Goẅgow they have a Rythm
(Scabbed Croik that sits on the Tree &c.) So many
times as it cryes, so many years will they live.

They foretell events by looking on the Shoulderbone of a Sheep. They have a care not to toutch it
with the Teeth or a Knife. They by it foretell
deaths, commotions, and tumultuary conventions
within the bounds.

They can let others see very strange things in
the Bone by setting their Foot on the persons
Foot, to whom they make the discovery. (? *mel.*)
The bone onely servs for that moon.

Some pretend to prophetic Inspirations and
foretel very fortuitous events. Their Responses
are deliver'd in very ambiguous Terms, so that
they are not known til the event. They call these
that have that Foresight *Fisich* i.e. *Sciens*. Such
persons are very reserv'd; and give not Answers

when asked but of their own Accord.

The SECOND SIGHT descends from Father to Son for some Generations. These who have it can prevent the Evil which doth threaten others, but cannot save themselves. It's so very troublsome to many, that theyd be gladly free from it. These persons observe that Spirits are great Lovers of Flesh and they see them some times taking flesh out of the pots, putting that which is worse in its place, of whilk they'l not taste.

These who have this foresight by compact give Responses being ask'd.

Sometymes they bring back to life these who are giving up the Ghost; but another dies in his place, and it always provs fatal.

They come (as some say) by the 2^d Sight thus: They look through the Knot of a piece of Tree and the boäls of sheers at a Southdoor upon a Burial as it passeth by.

RHAMANTA [ROMANCES]. When they'd have a Response there are four or more Sturdy persons who go to a Loch end, or a Kiln which hath two Doors; in which they cast a Cat alive backwards (*Edrych ymdhidhan Ithel a Gronw ynghylch bwrw câth i Gythrel*) [Look into the conversation of Ithel and Gronw about casting a cat to the Devil]. One of them goes under a Cauldron, a third invocats the Divel and a fourth faceth him. Sometimes there appear men with their heads in their hands. The Devil first asks somewhat, then they take the Cat and throw it at his Face. Then they ask the Devil and get answers, and obtain Requests, as the having meat, Lives prolong'd etc.

Editor's Notes

Cookoe was written by Lhuyd above *Gougous*, presumably the Scots word used in the original text (=gowkoo). The notion that it is unlucky to hear

36

the cuckoo while one is fasting is the subject of
a well-known saying in Gaelic:

Chuala mi chuthag gun bhiadh 'nam bhroinn,
Chunnaic ,mi 'n searrach 's a chùlaibh rium,
Chunnaic mi 'n t-seilcheag air lic luim,
'S dh'aithnich mi nach rachadh a' bhliadhn' ud liom.

'I saw the cuckoo without food in my stomach, I
saw the foal with his backside turned towards me,
I saw the snail on a bare flagstone, and I
recognised that yon year would not go well for
me.'

cp.Nicolson's *Gaelic Proverbs* p.144. In other
versions of this saying it is a stone-chat that is
seen on the bare flagstone, and the snail in a
hollow in the earth (*talamh toll*). See also
D.McPh. 196.

On the cuckoo as an omen of death, see Martin, 25,
and on St Kilda, 46-7, and J.G.C.(S) 256. See also
D.McPh. 196.

Airth = quarter of the globe

Corby = a raven. *They throw it meat* cp. ELSH 66,
where a similar statement in Welsh is quoted from
T.C.D. MS H.4.8, there incomplete owing to the MS
being torn.

Snayl in a base place, cp. the saying quoted above
under *cuckoo*.

pyots = magpies. *Folk* in the text is substituted
for *persons*. See ELSH 67: the reference to the
South here shows that this is a superstition of
the Borders, where magpies are common, not of the
Highlands, where they are rare.

Croik = dwarf. The asterisk at the beginning of
this sentence presumably refers it back to the
cuckoo at the beginning of this section.

the Shoulderbone of a Sheep: divination by gazing

37

at the shoulderblade of a sheep was called
slinneineachd in Gaelic. See Kirk 85; Pennant I
199, II 324; R.O. II 458; D.McPh. 193-4; J.G.C.(S)
263.

prophetic Inspirations: see J.G.C.(S) 269-276.

SECOND SIGHT: see e.g. Highland Papers I 167;
Martin 300-335; Pennant I 199, II 324; R.O. 463-
472; E.D.C. 362-365 (on St Kilda); J.G.C.(W) 120-
180; ST 1-92, 255-309; etc.

Spirits are great Lovers of Flesh: Kirk remarks
that many of the 'Scottish-Irish' will not taste
meat at funerals and banquets for this reason,
'lest they have Communion with, or be poysoned by,
them.' (p.69)

have this foresight by compact i.e. witches or
wizards who have acquired second sight by compact
with the Devil. Usually it was spontaneous, and as
such, defended vigorously against accusations that
it arose from such compacts.

another dies in his place cp. Kirk 78.

They come...by the 2^d Sight thus: Kirk says that
the would-be seer 'must run a Tedder of Hair
(which bound a Corps to the Bier) in a Helix about
his Midle from End to End; then bow his Head downwards, as did Elijah, I Kings 18.42., and look
back thorough his Legs untill he sie a Funerall
advance till the People cross two Marches; or look
this back thorough a Hole where was a Knot of Fir.'
He also gave directions for acquiring transient
second sight which are similar to those given here
in connection with the sheep's shoulderblade,
pp. 81-2.

boäls of sheers = the apertures in the handles of
scissors.

When they'd have a Response: for this barbarous
method of divination, see Martin 112; D.McPh. 197-9.

38

Taighghoirm na'n Caht; J.G.S.(S) 304-311.
J.Gregorson Campbell says that the ceremony was
known as 'giving his supper to the devil', and
that in Highland tradition there had only been
three persons who had dared to perform it.

9. THEIR BARDS

The Bardi of old were men of Acute Spirits skil-
full in Genealogies and poesy whose office was to
record in poesy the Acts of Valorous men and their
Genealogies: and for this they had a portion of
Land assign'd them. Now they are such whom we call
jockies which go up and down using Rythmes and
Satyrs and are plentifully rewarded.

Editor's Notes

jockies = strolling minstrels.

A short paragraph follows here in the MS, on sub-
ordinate clans that depend on ancient families as
their chiefs. This seems totally out of place in
a section devoted to Bards, and I have transferred
it to Section 21 on *Their Deference and Regard to
Some Persons*.

On the Bards, see Martin 102-104, 115-116, 200;
R.O. II 389-410.

10. THEIR WARRS AND ARMOUR

When they goe upon any martial Expedition whoever
first occur to them men or beast they kil it thô
never so innocent, if it be not of their party.
This is in the land of their enemy Mr Beaton. They
eat before they goe upon any hazard, otherwise if
they be killed fasting, they think they will
always trouble people in their dreams by appearing
to them.

Some of them have charms against all manner of
weapons but their own.

In fighting they think he wins the day that
gives the first wound.

Of old they used Bow, Sword, two-handed Swords,
Mailcoats, Head-pieces* Loch Aber axes* and that
which they called *Scapul* which covered their
Shoulders, Shield of Oak and Willow Wands, narrow
below and broad above. Targets made of Oak covered
with bull-hyde of an orbicular Form, Durks, and
Skeens.

Now they have most in use Guns, pistols, Sword,
Durk Target which they also carry along to church
and wear also an Head-piece.

The chief Families wear Shields of Steel. There
are Hereditary Offices of War assign'd to under-
families. The Head of ane Family hath commonly ane
Armour Bearer who goes in his Full Armour before
his Master, intervening betwixt him and all Hazard
in tyme of Warr.

This is calld *Galloglach*.

In the South anciently they us'd Gurk [*sic*] and
Spear, Sword, Gantlet and Steel Caps call'd Bonnet.

Editor's Notes

they kil it thô never so innocent: cp. Martin,
102-3.

On the Highland way of fighting, see Martin 210.

On Highland weapons, see Pennant I 211.

target = a small shield, made as described.

Hereditary Offices of War, see Martin 103-4.

Galloglach: cp. Martin 104. The term was originally used of Hebridean mercenaries engaged by the Irish chiefs in the middle ages.

11. THEIR FEUDS

There are a great many Feuds among them. There are
two Clans viz. the MacGregors and Buchanans who
have had endlesse Feuds one with another. The
first occasion of it was the killing of a black
sheep, to revenge which they have killed now one
and then another every one striving to be even
with one another, so that now the MacGregoirs have
killed 20 and the Buchanans 21.*

To keep up the Feuds they erect a Cairn of
Stones in the place where their Friend was killed,
calling it by his name. There also they draw a
deep Crosse there so they may be kept in mynde to
be reveng'd.

The Crosse is call(ed) Krosh Folliocht. [*Crois
folachd*].

Whoever of the Clan cometh that way they repair
the Crosse. Its calld *Crosse Failleacht*, the
Crosse of Feud or Enmity. Married women will take
part with their Kinred against their own Husband[s], and will upbraid them very tartly.

There are great animosities 'twixt' the Campbels and Mac-Donalds, the Mac orquodils and their
dependants side with the Campbels; all the rest
of the Macks side with the MacDonalds.

In the South formerly there were great Feuds
'twixt' the Johnsons, and Maxwells, the Kers and
Turnbulls.

*prŷn ai devaid ai dynion

Editor's Notes

On Highland feuds, see Burt II 9-12. Burt describes these cairns erected to keep up the
memories of clan battles. See also R.O. II 496-7.

prŷn ai devaid ai dynion = whether sheep or men?

12. THEIR FLITTING*

When they are flitting; if their carriage fall off the Horse they think it an ill omen.

When they goe Southward they flit on Munday, and when Northwards on Saturday.

In the place wither they go they kindle a Fire before their kine enter upon its marches.

'The first coag of Water they bring in, they put rushes therin. They have no will that another should come in their steed, til they be gone least some mischance should befall them.

In the South they flit on Fryday calld flitting Fryday.

The first thing they take into their House is Salt; then meal and Bear.

Editor's Notes

When they goe Southward: the saying connected with this custom is well known, but as recorded by Nicolson in Gaelic Proverbs p. 210, J.G.C.(W) 293, and FFSU 34, the northward flitting should be on the Saturday, the southward one on a Monday.

coag = a wooden vessel for holding milk etc.

bear = bere, four-rowed barley.

13. THEIR HOSPITALITY

They are generally very hospitable. Strangers may
travail amongst them gratis. When a Stranger comes
they direct him to an house which is design'd on
purpose for that use, and they send him his
Victuals plentifully. Snuff is useful amongst
them to make acquaintance.

If the Stranger be an Acquaintance or person of
Account, they send or go themselvs to attend him.
When the number of Strangers is great, then the
people contribute for provision to them which is
called *Coinaeh* [*Coinmheadh*] .i. common.

Gentlemen are very charitable to their poor:
some will have 20 or moe every meal in the house.

Editor's Notes

On Highland hospitality, see *e.g.* Martin 100;
Pennant II 401; R.O. II 397-399.

14. THEIR MONUMENTS

There are a great many high Stones by the way side
4 or 5 or moe in a circle, the biggest looketh
towards the East. Some alledge them to be the
Burial places of the Giants: others the Giants
Finger-stones which were casten from the Hills.
Others, the places where the Culdees conven'd:
others, Obelisks set up in memory of some Skirmish
or Battel. Others, places where Hunters met to
divide theyr prey. Others, Boundaries of Land.
Others, the places where pagans sacrific'd. On
high Hills there are Vestiges of great Bulwarks of
very big dry stones, so big as four oxen can not
draw. These they say, were the Habitation of
Giants who were the Attendants of Fin Mac Cûil,
who is a Famous Giant in Boeth.

There are places of great distance calld the
Gyants jump: some of which are Twixt hil and hil.

In I columb kil there is a broad Stone with a
hole in it; every one going there, turns the
bullet about; and the prophecy goeth that when the
Stone is worn through, then cometh Doomsday.

Queen Vyonar (Gwenhwyvar) wife to Arthur King
of the Britans about the year 500 falling into
Disgrace on Suspicion of Adultery was condemn'd to
be torn by Dogs; but escaping she fled into Scotland dying on a Hill of Stormond (where she had
liv'd some time) she was buryed at Meigle in
Perthshire. About three miles from the Hill, where
she is buried there is a Stone higher than a man
with her picture and dogs tearing in one side, and
on the other men pursuing her. There's an other
Grave stone where her servants were— her Servants
were buried.

In Galloway ther's the Burial place of King
Galdus or Gallus the first who did fight with the
Romans. It is neare Wigton circl'd with 13 great
Stones and two in the midle.

They have some big stones here and there the

46

occasions wherof is not known.

Editor's Notes

Giants Finger-stones, see Boswell 261.

Fin Mac Cuil = Fionn Mac Cumhail, leader of the band of heroes called Fiantaichean. See *e.g.* Martin 152, 217, 219-220; J.G.Campbell, *The Fians* (London, 1891); Reidar Christiansen, *The Vikings in Gaelic Tradition* (Oslo, 1931); Gerard Murphy, Introduction to Part 3 of *Duanaire Finn* (Irish Texts Society, vol. XLIII); SSU 1-31, 209-214; etc.

Boeth: (Boethius) = Hector Boece, the early sixteenth century Scottish historian (see H.B. 62).

I Columb Kil = Iona.

bullet = boulder. This is referred to by Pennant, II 289. 'A little North-West of the door of the chapel is the pedestal of a cross: on it are certain stones, that seem to have been the support of a tomb. Numbers who visit this island (I suppose the ELECT impatient for the consummation of all things) think it incumbent on them to turn each of these trice round, according to the course of the sun. They are called *Clacha-bràth*; for it is thought that the *brath* or end of the world, will not arrive till the stone on which they stand is worn through.'

Queen Vyonar: the tradition about this sculptured stone goes back to Hector Boece's *History of Scotland* (1527) and presumably earlier. See *The Sculptured Stones of Scotland* I 22-24, and plates LXXIII, LXXIV, and LXXV; O.S.A. I 506-7; E.C.M. 297.

See also MacFarlane's *Geographical Collections*, III 222, in an anonymous undated (probably seventeenth century) account of Stormont and Gowrie:

'Monuments and remarkable things in this Countrey are the Stones at Meigle cut with several Figures and Hieroglyphicks said to be the Burial-place of Queen Vandora, who had her Dwelling three miles North upon a Hill called Barray. The Ruines yet remain, and shew it to have been a huge Building of stone.'

15. MUSIC

The Greatest Music is Harp, Pipe, Viol, and Trump.
Most part of the Gentry play on the Harp.

Pipers are held in great Request so that they
are train'd up at the Expence of Grandees and have
a portion of Land assignd and are design'd such a
man's piper. Their women are good at vocal music;
and inventing of Songs.

Lhuyd's Notes (Folios 29-30)

They have Quern Songs and rowing songs for sea.
The Boat sings [sic] they call irraim [iorraim].
Kronan [cronan] is a raucous Song; Lwiniyg
[luinneag] a melodious chearfull song. Awbhran
[Amhran] (or Ôran [òran]) any grave serious song.

Editor's Notes

On the music of the Highlanders, see Kirk 108;
Martin 14, 199-200; Martin St Kilda 73; Pennant,
I 215-6, II 348-350; R.O. 412-414; Necker de
Saussure, III 444-461; MacCulloch, 396-451;
Frances Tolmie; FFSU; HF; etc.

There are many allusions to the instruments
mentioned here, in the Gaelic poetry of the seventeenth century.

On the importance of pipers, see Burt II 65-66.

16. THEIR FEASTS

They are very carefull that the Servants of those who feast with them be so intoxicated with drink that they must be carryed out to their Bed on Barrows. They never give over til all the Drink be Spent. Tho they drink never so much they must drink at the Doors; and this they call *Deoch an dorus*, the drink of the door.

Editor's Notes

On drinking customs, see Martin 106.

17. THEIR FARMERS

Generally tenants are oblig'd to all Carriage and
Arage, at all times when they are called. They are
Lyable in some places to pay all Impositions and
public Burdens, and commonly the one half.
   They are to attend their Masters at Hosting
(i.e. war*ing) Hunting and Stenting.*
   Besides their paying of Duties and presents
they pay also good Wills.
   They are generally wont to entertain their
Masters whole Family for a day to two once a year,
which was called *Kwyd eihie*, [*Cuid oidhche*] i.e.
the Nights entertainment, which is yet in use in
some places. Others have converted it into money.
When Strangers come to their Master's House they
send a great deal of Good Will.
   They contribute towards the portion of their
Master's eldest daughter.

Editor's Notes

areage = servitude due by tenants in men and
horses to their landlords.

stenting = assessment for taxation.

goodwill = (here) gratuitous supplies.

they contribute, cp. Martin 210.

18. THEIR TRYING OFFENCES

They bore a hole in a Tree and cause the person
whom they suspect to put in his Finger, and they
drive in a wedge to extort confession; in some
place they cause Fornicators ride the meer, tying
some weights to their Feet
    When any contest falleth out, their most ancient
and usual way is to choose 2 or 3 Arbitrators of
equal degree on a side, and they ordinarly healf
the matter in debate betwixt the parties.

Editor's Notes

They bore a hole in a Tree: there are two standing
stones on Canna, each called *Clach a' Pheanais*,
the Punishment Stone, with holes of a similar size,
said to have been used for this purpose.

meer = mare; but the last letter is uncertain;
could be *c*.

healf = Scots *half* vb., to halve? The reading is
uncertain.

19. PLOUGHING, HARROWING, DUNGING THE GROUND

They plough onely with Horse[s] of which four goe
in a breast *viz. in Ila and elswhere* and two, next
to the plough. In some places he who leads the
Horses goeth back always and Strikes the Horses on
the Face.

In may places they delve more than they til,
and they carry the muck on their backs in a Criel.

Some when they yoak first Sprinkle the Horses
with Urine.

They begin nothing without saying In the name
of the Father, Son and Holy Ghost.

In some places they tye the Harrow to the
Horse tayl.

When they go to plough folding they make pot-
tage and butter there. The first spoonfull they
take and hide in a Furrow of the Foldings.

Editor's Notes

They plough onely with Horses: in the north east-
ern part of Scotland at this time ploughing was
done with oxen.

in Ila and elswhere: this was added by Lhuyd. In
O.S.A. (1794) the minister of Kilchoman in Islay
wrote that 'Our manner of husbandry requires also
a good many horses, 4 being yoked in each plough'
(XI 279).

Burt (II 41) wrote that 'Where the soil is deeper
they plough with four of their little horses
abreast. The Manner this:- Being thus ranked they
are divided by a small space into pairs, and the
driver, or rather leader, of the plough having
placed himself before them, holding the two inner-
most by their heads to keep the couples asunder,
he with his face toward the plough, goes backward,
observing, through the space between the horses,

the way of the ploughshare.

Criel = a basket carried on the back. The *delving* was done in such places with the *cas-chrom*, which survived in remote places until recently. See FFSU 3, and photograph 4a. The *muck* in places near the sea was often seaweed.

Some...first sprinkle cp. Pennant I 206.

they tye the Harrow: Burt comments on this 'barbarous custom', II 43.

folding = outfield which had been manured by cattle being folded on it.

20. CLER SHEANCHAN

The *Cler Sheanchan* were a Company of itinerant
poets who went along Gentlemen's Houses, giving
Account of their Genaalogies, and as they were rewarded return'd either a Satyr or Panegryric.
Their Reflecions were either mystic call'd *Cam-Ran*
or playn and evident call'd *Dan direach*.

Editor's Notes

Cler Sheanchan = Cliar Sheanchain. See the article
on Senchan's Company by W.J.Watson, *Celtic Review*
IV 80-87. The term is a very ancient one, going
back to the late sixth century. Senchan was the
successor of Dallan Forgaill, the leader of the
poets of Ireland at the time of the convention of
Drum Ceatt in 575, when St Columba saved them from
banishment which was sought because of the burden-
someness of their exactions.

The Scottish government sought to suppress the
itinerant Gaelic poets in the sixteenth and early
seventeenth centuries, probably because they represented the intellectual class of Gaeldom and
encouraged Gaelic separatism.

See also Angus MacLeod, *The Songs of Duncan Ban
MacIntyre*, note to line 890.

Cam-ran, not found in Scottish Gaelic dictionaries,
is defined in Dinneen's Irish-English dictionary
as 'a crooked or faulty stanza, an epigrammatic or
satirical verse; the reply to such.' The usual
contrast is between *Dàn Dìreach*, syllabic verse in
strict metres with assonance and alliteration, and
amhrán (*òran*) or verse in stressed metre with
vowel rhymes only. It appears that the term *dàn
dìreach* was losing its original significance in
the Highlands in Kirkwood's time. Armstrong's

dictionary has *cam-dhằn*, 'iambic verse', presumably = verse in stressed metre.

21. THEIR DEFERENCE AND REGARD TO SOME PERSONS

After meat they pray for their Chief and the King, naming the Chief first. Some also pray for their Superiors and Benefactors.

They have a Relation which is called *coaltus* [*comhdhaltas*] from *Coalo* [? *comhaladh*], which is 'twixt the Children of the Foster Child, and the Nurse's Children which continueth to the 20th Generation. They reckon a Foster Brother dearer to a man than his own Brother and will dye for one an other.

They reckon him their chief, whom they choose for their patron: tho he be not of their name. They'l ingage for their chief against all, deadly.

Every considerable ancient family hath Clans who depend of them owning these for Chief; and when they die, they leav the Chief a Legacy. Some families will have seven or eight of these Clans, who give a Bond of Fealty unto the Chief.

When they are a dying they leave a Legacy to their Chief, a *Collopy* [*colpa*] viz. the best horse *eih-kollopy* [*each-colpa*] or cow etc. according to their wealth in retaliation of which the Chief giveth to their Eldest Son a Sword, or Gun or both when he comes to years.

When tenents dye they leive the best Cattel which they have to their Master called *Damh iwrsin* [*Damh ursainn*] The Door Ox. They have very few Titles of Honour.

Editor's Notes

Every considerable ancient family: this paragraph occurs at the end of Section 9 on 'Their Bards' in the MS, but it so obviously belongs here that I have transferred it.

The Door Ox: so called because it was the best

beast, kept nearest the door. Kirkwood implies
that this was a voluntary legacy, but the fact is
that on a tenant's decease his heirs had to give
his best horse or cattle beast to the landlord or
the tacksman, a burdensome exaction. See Martin
114-5, and GWSU under EACH URSAINN.

22. THEIR FUEL

Their fewel is piets, turf, Firwood &c. They have
no coals but in Cantyre and one of the West Isles.
 For fire tongues the Countrey people use a
piece of Forked wood. For Candles in many places
they use the Roots of Firs. In other places they
use Ruffies which are made of wrought Tallow
compass'd about with a clean rag. Some fill the
weason of a Ship with melted Tallow, pushing a weik
into it which gives great light. The Gentry use a
Candle 3 qrs. long.
 In the Isles they make the Candles of the Oyle,
which they take from the melts of Fishes, and for
a wyke they use rushes; some use the Oyl of Herr-
ing Guts.
 Gentlemen who use Fir Candles have a man who
servs for a candlstick, holding it perpetually in
his hand.

Editor's Notes

On fir candles, see the articles on 'Peer-Men and
their Relations' by James Linn and Mary MacKellar
in the *Celtic Magazine*, VIII 556 and IX 45.

one of the West Isles: probably Mull: see Pennant
II 408.

Ruffies = wicks clogged with tallow.

weason of a ship = gullet of a sheep.

weik = wick.

melt = spleen. Actually the oil was usually made
from the livers of fishes, particularly of saithe.

23. FIRE AND SALT

They reckon Fire and Salt hallow'd things. They
cast fire after such as goes about any work as
Hunting, Fishing &c. When they renew Children's
Cloaths, they let a litle coal of Fire fall
through them thrice.

If any beast taste of their meat, they circle
the dish with Fire. When they suspect a witch to
have been in the House, they cast fire after her.

If a beast be torn they'l not take it into
their house, till they spinkle it with Salt or
Ashes; and this they doe if a beast fall over a
Rock; when they make it ready they give the first
piece of it to a dog.

For Salt in some places they use an Herb pulveriz'd.

Editor's Notes

hallow'd things: there is a well-known Gaelic
proverb to the effect that 'the stealing of salt,
seed of plants, and lint make the thief liable to
judgment without mercy'. See J.G.C.(S) 236.

torn = damaged.

an Herb pulveriz'd: possibly a kind of seaweed,
see the last paragraph of Section 7.

24. THEIR HUNTING

When one goeth a hunting, any who hate him take a
Bone of some Beast which he had taken formerly
putting it into a Tree, thinking that so long as
it sticks there he'll never come speed. When they
go a hunting if a woman passe by on their left
hand, they think they'l not luch.

If one go out to hunt Venison for the use of
any man in particular, and easily find it, they
say that such a person is Fey and will not live
long; but if it be found with difficulty he'l live
long.

Editor's Notes

For hunting in the Highlands in the old days, see
e.g. Pennant I 121-3; R.O. 403-4.

come speed = succeed.

luch, probably = luck, vb., to prosper.

Fey, see ELSH 67.

25. BUYING AND SELLING

In buying a Horse the Seller holds him by the Bridle without and the Buyer within with a wisp in his hand, which the seller giveth him going sun-gate about.

When this is done they go to a *Tavarn* (i.e. Alehouse) and taking a cake or Bannok, they put them into as many plyes as they can; and the Buyer takes three Bitles. They think it a good omen if a horse dungs in tyme of buying but if he pisse they'l not medle with him. ? *mel*.

They seek a cautioner for suspected Goods. When they compleate one an other in their conditions they say his soul get the odds who ever wants it.

Editor's Notes

On selling a horse in the Highlands, see R.O. II 450.

sungate = sunwise, *deiseal* in Gaelic.

plyes = folds.

bitles = little bits.

? *mel*: see p.108

26. FISHING AND SHIPPING

When they goe to sea they use a certain Short
Form of Prayer. The Skipper sayth blesse the Ship.
One answers God the Father blesse her. The Skipper
sayth again blesse the Ship: Answr. God the Son
blesse her. Then he asks what do you fear? one
answers nothing God the Father being with us, &c.
Then the Skipper prayeth that he that preserv'd
the Israelites in the red sea, and Jonas and Paul
&c. may blesse them: and so they conclude with the
Lord's Prayer.

Before they put a Boat to sea, they kil a Goat
upon its rudder, thereby hoping for the better
Successe. *This is when they wait a Fair wind; and
then they chop off the head at one stroak; others,
kill it at the bow.*

When a ship is in Hazard they boro a piece of
money which they give to the first poor Body they
meet with and pray for the Ship. *They name the
person at sea, when they boro* [?] *the money.* They
say also to one an other Keep a good heart and
patience, the Night is coming; wherin all Fayth-
full men pray for all distressed men at Sea we
will then get Relief.

In the Western Isles they get a Gale of Wind
ordinarily. When they Fish with a line and a Bait
they spit on the Bait, thinking otherwise they
will not speed.

The first fish they take they say this is a
Little Fish *Brianan* and putting its head into
their mouth chew it. They do not count their Fish.
They have a Charm wherby to get plenty themselvs
and hinder others.

Lhuyd's Notes (Folio 30)

When people are windbound they erect a *Templ
Chleaman* [*Teampull Chliamain*] i.e. 2 or 3 foot of
clods and stones in form or a Buylding and put up

63

in it a rag on a stick representing a Mast: the
face of the Sail towards the Airth they desire
the wind. This is usd in the Hebrides espec. when
they want a northerly wind, Clement being patron
of the Herries.

At Teampyl Chynih [*Teampull Choinnich*] in Y
Colym Kil [Iona] hard by Knock an Riddiyr [*Cnoc
an Ridire*] theirs a Stone Trough calld Lossit
Kheynnih [*Losaid Choinnich*] or Kenneths Trough;
where the custome is that when they want a fair
wind, they cause a true Virgin empty out the water
of it, throwing it betwixt her legs backward; her
face being towards the aird from whence they want
the wind. And within 24 hours 'tis common to be
supply'd with the wind they want, prob. est. Mr
John Beaton.

Editor's Notes

a certain Short Form of Prayer: see Carswell,
240-1, from whose translation of John Knox's
Liturgy it was reproduced by Martin, with many
misprints, 127-130. The prayer survived into the
nineteenth century; see C.G. I 332-4, 'Urnuigh
Mhara' 'Sea Prayer', taken down by Alexander Carmichael from Gilleasbuig MacLellan, shipmaster,
North Lochboisdale, South Uist.

they kil a Goat upon its rudder: cp. Martin 109.
Martin says that it was 'an ancient custom among
the Islanders, to hang a He-Goat to the Boat's
Mast, hoping thereby to procure a Favourable Wind'.

speed = succeed.

*They have a Charm wherby to get plenty themselves
and hinder others*: this charm was called *sgiunach*,
see Neil MacAlpine's Gaelic Dictionary, where it
is defined as 'a charm or enchantment to enable
its possessor to get all the fish about a boat or
headland, while his less fortunate neighbours

64

stare with amazement'. Robert Kirk mentions it in
La. III 551, 'ther is another charm called *sgiunach*
that attracts the Fishes plentifully to the
Angler', see ICDF 410. Unfortunately this charm
seems to be lost.

the Herries i.e. Harris in the Outer Hebrides
(*Na Hearadh*). The interesting medieval church at
Rodel there is dedicated to St Clement.

a true Virgin empty out the water of it: this is
mentioned by E.D.Clarke, who visited Iona in 1797.
'A small stone coffin of red granite lay among the
broad leaves of the burdock, at the west end of
the cathedral. The poor lunatic [a man there who
had attached himself as guide] had torn away the
surrounding foliage, and insisted on my noticing
it. "If you want a north wind" said he, in a
whisper, "bring a virgin of eighteen, whose purity
has never been suspected, and bid her wash this
coffin. Then, when the virgin works, you'll hear
the north wind work."'
    Clarke adds a note that 'this extraordinary
superstition is implicitly believed among the
natives of the island' (I 315).

27. CHARMES

They use Charms for preventing diseases in man or beast and for curing them; and many other diseases.
They cure the Headake and Toothake by charms; †for preventing diseases in man and Beast and for curing them.†

† They cure the Headach and Toothach by Charms.†

There is a Family of the name of Stuart in Appin of Lorn which has a soveraign charm against the Fairies, which they communicate onely to their Offspring. The Charm they write on a piece of paper, the words are intermingl'd with Crosses. It is hung about the neck of the person affected. They call this charm the Gospell.

If they get the name of a person who has a mote in his eye, (thô at never so great a distance) by taking water into their Mouth and mumbling over the charm, they spit out the mote with the water. This water they will not set on the earth but on a Tree, when they bring it from the well. *Prob*[atus] *est Jo. Beaton.* [*It has been proved, according to John Beaton*]. *Coviwch y Glain Neidr a'r Ychelwydh.* [*Remember the Snake-stone and the Honeysuckle*].

They use the water of three boats for the Rickets and a charm with it.

Against the Evil Eye they use Salt and Ashes, and on the pronouncing the words they spit on the Salt and Ashes. *This is called Eppi er hwl* [*Obaidh air shùil*]. *They give this salt and water in a spoon to the person affected.*

Those who rage at some Fits and awake with Fury through their sleep once in two nights or offner who otherwise are well enough they say such are not babtiz'd or have not got enough of water. For cure of this they clap a Bible frequently on their Faces. *viz. they let the leaves fly with their thumbs and this they call Gy rwin leabhair* [*Gaoth roimh'n leabhar*].

They charm especially on the Lord's Day: and if it be a chronical Disease, they charm on the first

66

Sunday of the Quarter.

They have charms for Diseases of the Spleen,
Hepatic Diseases and evel eye which hurts what
they look on. They use to blesse first those who
have the Evel Eye to prevent the Danger.

They use against Witchcraft the Ran tree,
Kyrdhyne [*Caorthann*], especially when they go to
Sea. By charms they take away the Substance of
Milk. They use to charm Beasts with Words, Gems
and Herbs.

Christus vim verbis, vim gemmis, vim dedit
herbis.

On the third of May they take the Urine and
Dung of the Catle together with mans urine and
therwith they sprinkle their Catle; thinking this
an Antidose against all Charms and Divelrie.

For several Diseases they have sevl. Stones
called by Saints names: the principal is S^t.
Marie's nut.

The Elf Arrow is like a barbed Arrow of an
Orange colour, which they hang about the neck.

Lhuyd's Notes (Folios 30-31)

To cure a broken bone they take a Brier and
cleave it almost from one end to the other, and
put therein a Charm; viz. they speak three or four
words at the cleaving holding the rod to their
mouths at the utterance; then this brier they put
upon the wall above the sick person's bed; and as
the Rod joyns so will the Bone. Probat. est. J.
Beat.

To have a piece of iron which has been in the
fire to strike fire They say *Tephig qle qioch;
Tephig qioch qlê*; and *Tephig qle qiochy*.

Editor's Notes

For Scottish Gaelic charms and incantations

67

generally, see the six volumes of *Carmina Gadelica*, the collection of Alexander Carmichael. See also the paper on "Gaelic Incantations and Charms of the Hebrides" read by William MacKenzie to the Gaelic Society of Inverness on 23rd March 1892 (Transactions, XVIII 97-182; and J.G.C.(W) 54-107. For earlier references, see e.g. Kirk 108; A.S.M. I 68, 84, 153; Pennant II 245.

Toothake, cp. J.G.C.(W) 69-7).

Stuart in Appin, cp. J.G.C.(W) 293. The charm is given by Robert Kirk in La. III 551, see ICDF p. 430.

They call this charm the Gospell: see J.G.C.(W) 79, 94. This survived in the Appin district into the middle of the nineteenth century. In the archives of the R.C. Diocese of Argyll and the Isles there is a letter from the Rev Fr Archibald Chisholm, then a young priest, to Bishop Scott, written from Glencoe on 31st January 1840, saying that about a dozen Protestants had applied to him within the last fortnight for gospels. 'The fact is, however, that I am ignorant of how a gospel is given, to whom it should be given, and under what conditions it should be given, as I can find no mention of this practice in any of my books.' The 'gospels' were apparently wanted as cures for various illnesses, and the Bishop is asked what should be done in the circumstances. I am obliged to the Rev Fr R.MacDonald, now parish priest of Dunoon, for drawing my attention to this letter. William MacKenzie (TGSI XVIII 152*n*) quotes Croker (*Fairy Legends*, p. 360), who says that "a 'gospel' is a text of Scripture written in a peculiar manner, and which has been blessed by a priest. It is sewed in red cloth, and hung around the neck as a cure or preventive against various diseases." Kirk says the Stuart of Appin charm was against falling evil and palsy.

clap a Bible frequently on their Face: Martin describes how his Bible was borrowed on Colonsay to fan the face of a patient suffering from a fever, p. 248. Fr Allan McDonald tells how this was done to cure a person of having second sight, S.T. 291.

first Sunday of the Quarter, cp. Kirk 69.

Ran = rowan. See R.O. II 454; J.G.C.(W) 11-12.

take away the Substance of Milk: cp. Kirk 71; Martin 120-122; S.T. 322-3.

gems: Gaelic *leug*. See Martin 134; Pennant II 266; R.O. 452-454; Clarke I 298-300.

Urine: cp. R.O. 454-5; J.G.C.(S) 49; J.G.C.(W) 11, 14.

St Marie's nut: in Gaelic, *àirne Muire*. This is a kind of bean (*Mucuna urens* or *Dioclea reflexa*) brought to the shores of the Hebrides and the north-west of Scotland by the Gulf Stream, rarely found and considered lucky. See Martin, 12, 38, 116; Pennant II 266; FFSU 13; GWSU under ÀIRNE MOIRE.

Elf Arrow: these are of flint, which is not common in the Highlands. See Kirk 69, 76-8; Pennant I 116; J.G.C.(S) 26, 154.

Christus vim verbis: 'Christ gave strength to charms, to gems, and to herbs'.

Tephig gle gioch: it is obvious from the underdotting that Lhuyd was uncertain of the Gaelic expression he heard. The first two words might be for *Tapadh gléidh*, 'Good luck keep..' but the meaning of the third word is uncertain.

28. DISEASES AND PHYSIC

They are not much troubled with any Diseases but
feavours; wherof they die commonly. The women are
subject to headaches. *They abhor physic and
bloudletting and so they have few or no physicians*.
Their Catholicon is Aq[u]a Vitæ either alone or
with Butter and Honey. They retain a prescription
from a Tramontan Doctor, such as they call *Olluiv*
[*Ollamh*] viz. *Oliyv Ilaih* [*Ollamh Ileach*] which is
to keep the Head Feet and Heart warm and to be
blythe and innocent.

They think that there are Superfluities and
Extremities in every man's Body that would cure
every Disease of the same Body: if there were Skil
to make, temper and apply them; e.g. the Hair,
Nails, Urin, Spitle etc. which are Antidotes for
any poyson. *This M.[r] Beaton says is a practise but
of late years.*

They think he who suffers much payn in his
Body here by long sicknesse, is on purpose put on
that Pennance by Almighty God, that the Body it-
self (which onely sins say they) may suffer and
satisfy for its own sins, and so purg'd purely go
to Heaven. *This is an Ecclesiastic Doctrine of
Pennance etc. Mr Beaton.*

They say that where one dies of a Consumption,
if any Friends be in the room at [the] expiring
the same Disease will stil seize one of them. *Q.*

Lhuyd's Notes (Folio 31)

*Arver yr hen vedhygon gynt yn yr ycheldir oedh:
lhadh gwaed ar y kleigion a phigæ* Echinus marinus
orviculatus. [= Formerly the custom of the old
doctors in the Highlands was: to let the blood of
a sick person with the spines of the sea urchin.]

The Highlanders as other nations are subject to
Apoplexies, Epilepsies, Phrensies, and Mania,
Hypochrondria, Rheumatisms, K[ing's] Evil, very

70

common, Bohem, Squinancy, in abundance; also
Apostens, Exulcerations of the Lungs, Pleurisies
&c. Phthisis, peripneumonia, Consumptions, in
short all Diseases incident to other nations. They
have the Pa[l]sies oft as also sorts of Dropsies
and Fluxes but the Gout is very rare among them.

Editor's Notes

They abhor physic and bloudletting: this sentence
has been deleted in the MS, probably on the advice
of the Rev John Beaton, who was himself the
descendant of the most famous medical family of
the Highlands and Islands. He is also probably
responsible for the information contained in
Lhuyd's notes to this section.

Tramontan = Highland. The word is used in the
identical sense by Kirk, *Secret Commonwealth* pp.
72, 106, and the second title-page of the MS La.
III 551 version contains the words 'among the
Tramontaines or Sctoish-Irish' (Rossi, 259).

Olluiv [*Ollamh*] = a master of science, professor,
doctor. Two famous members of the Beaton family,
brothers, were called the *Ollamh Ìleach* 'Islay
Doctor' and the *Ollamh Muileach* 'Mull Doctor'. See
G.MSS.S. 309; J.G.C.(S) 285-6.

*to keep the Head Feet and Heart warm and to be
blyth and innocent*: this advice was still remember-
ed at the end of the eighteenth century. The Rev
Dugal Campbell, in his account of the united
parish of Kilfinichen and Kilviceuen written for
the *Old Statistical Account of Scotland* (1795) remarked that:

'Since the Reformation, the parish has pro-
duced none eminent for learning, if we except
the Beatons of Pennicross, who were doctors of
physic. The family is now extinct; but they are

71

still spoken of in the country with admiration
for their skill in physic. It is said, that one
of them was sent for to attend one of the kings
of Scotland; and that the people of the country
flocked to him for advice as to their health,
during his absence, when he gave them this short
rule: "To be cheerful, temperate and early
risers" [*Bhith gu sùgach, geanmnaidh, mochair-
each*]. They had a large folio MS in Gaelic,
treating of physic, which was left with a woman,
the heiress of the Beatons, and seen by some now
living; but what became of it, the incumbent,
after all his inquiries, could not find. It is
perhaps lost, as the heirs of this woman are
quite illiterate.'   (O.S.A. XIV 204-5).

For notes on the Beaton Gaelic medical MSS, see
ELSH 42-44. See also H.Cameron Gillies, *Regimen
Sanitatis* and G.MSS.S. 1-71. Martin gives a long
account of diseases prevalent, and cures used, in
Skye in his time, 175-199, and also refers to
these subjects in his accounts of other islands.

This is an Ecclesiastic doctrine of penance: it is
in fact the Roman Catholic doctrine of purgatory.

Bohem (?) = (reading doubtful).

Apostens = abcesses.

29. MUSIC

†The greatest music is harp, pipe, viol and trump.
Most part of the gentry play on the harp. Pipers
are held in great request. They are train'd up at
the expence of Grandees and have a portion of Land
assignd them and are design'd such among pipers.
  †Their women are good at vocal music and inventing songs.

Editor's Notes

Deleted in the MS; this Section is identical
with No. 15.

30. ANENT THUNDER

They are exceedingly affrighted with Thunder and
Lightning. At that time they shut their windows.

†The Commons think that Thunder is a Fight
between ane old man and ane old wife, beating one
an other with a Budget full of Air†. *Ni vynne M*.
B. adel hyn [*Mr Beaton would not allow this*]. A
Budget is a Skin sew'd together wherein they use
to put their meal.

In time of Lightning they use to put iron into
the fire: fearing otherwise the conflagration of
their houses; or they cover their Fire with the
Gridiron. In the South they think that thunder
breaks upon any thing that is red and therefore at
that tyme such who have any red thing upon them
hide it. When the Fire (*in Lightning time*) is
without [the] house they cover it.

Editor's Notes

they shut their windows: not many of the Highlanders had houses with windows that could be opened
and shut at this time.

The Commons think: this sentence is crossed out in
the MS, and the significant remark *Ni vynne M. B.
adel hyn* in Welsh inserted = Mr Beaton would not
allow this. Significant because it suggests that
other deletions in Lhuyd's transcript may well
have been made on the Rev John Beaton's advice.

they use to put iron into the fire: cp. J.G.C.(S)
235.

31. CALLING PERSONS BY THEIR NAMES

In the night time they will not call upon children by their name, least the Devil get power over
them. When persons of elder years are called on in
the night by their name, they'l not answer unlesse
they be called 3 times, fearing that it is a
Spirit.

Editor's Notes

Cp. Fr Allan McDonald IV 26: 'If a knock come
to a door after midnight it is not right to
answer it or say *"Thig a staigh"* "Come in." Wait
till the knock is repeated and then ask "Who is
there?"

32. THIGGING

To thig is to beg assistance of Friends which is
very ordinary among persons of every Quality. Men
thig Horses and corn; women thig cows, sheep and
goats. When a person of Quality thigs he is attended with a great many servants, whereof one is the
Spokesman and intimates to the Master of the House
the end of their coming. By this means they get a
great deal of one kind and other.

When young men of the common sort are to plenish
they thig corn, both in Seed time and harvest.
Sometimes great persons onely send Letters, with
one or other to receive their good will.

Editor's Notes

There is a poem on the inconvenience caused by
this well-known custom in the Book of the Dean of
Lismore, *Mór an feidhm freagairt na bhfaighdheach*
'To answer the demands for aid .. is a great
effort', see W.J.W. 67. Hugh MacDonald, historian
of the MacDonalds, describes the thigging of
Domhnall Gallda, H.P. I 56. See also Martin, 78-9;
Burt, II 107; GWSU, under FAOIGHEADH.

good will = gratuity, gift.

33. BIRTH AND BAPTISM

A woman with child *when she sees a Hare or steps over a Hair rope* slits up a litle of her petticoat to prevent Hareshaw *i.e. least they* [sic] *child should prove Hairlip'd*.

When a Male is born they put a sword or knife in his hand, and a spindle *or a Rock i.e. Distaff* into the hand of a female.

When they are carried out to be baptiz'd they cast a litle Fire after them; v.g. a litle coal, straw etc.

Instead of Butter saps they mix meal and Ale together; which every person at the Feast must taste in order. *This may be p'haps in the South.* They put a piece of iron on the bottom of the Cradle, that no evil eye wrong the Child. *Q.*

In Badzenoch, LochAber etc the Midwife or any one that can read, baptizeth dipping the child in cold water, naked with some Form of Words. Their Gossips and Comers take the Child in their Arms after Baptism and promise in the Child's name. Yet some such will be rebaptizd at 17 or 18 years of age by a minister.

A lad born on Sunday they call Donald, a lass Jennet. *This can be but in some places.*

When they come from Church at their eating in the House they put the Child into a Basket full of Bread and Cheese, and then take him out. All who enter must eat thereof and then take a Drink. *Probly in the S. Countrey.*

At the end of the Feast the Nurse or Midwife, gives the Child to the Godfather or Godmother who name their Gift to the Child viz. a cow, meer etc. and then the Child is given round about and every one bestoweth a Gift, all which the parents undertake to preserve for the use of the Child. The Laws of Godfather and Godmother, of Gossips and Cummers are strictly observed in conscientiously. They'l not marry any of the Gossip Relation, more than they were Parents and children. *This the Romans observe.*

For Physic they pour a litle ꞌUrin down their throats in a morning to make them excrete.

They put the meat out of their own mouths into the childs. For about a year they use to wash their children in cold water evening and morning. Before they wash the Child they dip their Finger thrice and put it into the child's mouth. *This says M.B. is after washing.* They use Wollen Cloaths about their children.

Til six or seaven years they suffer not their children to wear Shoe or Stoken.

Few of the children of the Commons are taught to read.

The Bairns are taught the Lord's Prayer, Belief and Ten commandmands.

Lhuyd's Note (Folio 31)

Universally of old and in some places at this day in the Highlands the Gossip takes the Child and holding it on his arm he stands at the door holding the childs hand so as to be over the threshold and then pours on water sayin[g] *Nomine patris et Filii et Sp. sancti*; I baptiz thee A.

A child born and christend on the Sabb: day, will never take the plague.

Editor's Notes

There is remarkably little about baptismal customs in the early accounts of the Highlands and Islands, but see Martin, St. Kilda 91.

Hareshaw = hairlip.

Rock = distaff. The word, being inserted between two lines, is rather difficult to read.

a litle fire, cp. R.O. 423.

sap = 'pieces of bread soaked or boiled in milk
(etc.)... often given as food to children' (S.N.D.).

meer = a mare.

Gossips and Comers (= cummers), i.e. sponsors and
godparents.

the Midwife or any one that can read, baptizeth:
this is interesting evidence of the persistence of
lay baptism in the Highlands, where it was very
much disapproved of by the Presbyterian ministers,
as undermining their authority (it would often be
practised by Catholic and Episcopalian recusants)
and depriving them of their dues. Thus in 1656 the
Argyll Synod Minutes record that 'one Manis mc
Raink, shoemaker in Ulva, that he did baptise a
child to an other man, took on him, being a poore
ignorant mane, to administrat the sacrament, ane
odious thing to midle with holy things without a
call, Therfore the synod appoints the presbyterie
of Lorne to cite him before them, and being
judicially convicted, that they deall with him and
hold out unto him the nature of the sine, and the
punishment due to such a sine even in this world,
and much more in that which is to come, And that
the presbyterie apoint him to apaire publickly in
every church within the presbytrie that he may be
ane example to others.' (A.S.M. II 127-8).

In October the Rev. Robert Dunconson, minister
of Dalavich in Argyllshire, who had been sent by
the Synod to the Catholic districts of Ardnamur-
chan, Sunart, Moydart and Arisaig for two months
during the preceding summer to "travell among
these places, preaching and catechiseing and in-
structing them" (i.e., bringing them into line)
'having reported severall abuses in these places
particularly parents not holding up their own
children to baptisme from a corrupt principall, in
causeing other privat persons baptize their child-

ren or doing it themselves when they want
ministers, putting salt in the water used in
baptisme, which is much occasioned by the over-
sight and inadvertency of the ministers of the
presbyterie of Sky adjacent to them', the Synod
ordered that letters be written to the Presbytery
of Skye and to Cameron of Lochiel 'to rectifie
the said abuses'. (A.S.M. 201-202).

Putting salt into the water of baptism at
private baptisms was probably a memory of the
Catholic practice of the priest putting salt into
the child's mouth as a sign that he is to be freed
from the corruption of sin. The Catholic Church,
of course, has always allowed lay baptism in cases
of necessity.

There is an interesting description of lay
baptism in the Highlands in the seventeenth century in a MS account of the mission of the Rev
James Devoyer and the Rev James Cahassy in the
papers of the late Monsignor Cameron:

'A curious circumstance is related at this
time i.e. [around 1686]. Permission had formerly
been given for lay baptism "in periculo mortis"
[in danger of death], when neither priest nor
missionary was at hand. This had come to be extended and abused. Even without the risk of
imminent death, baptisms were occasionally ad-
ministered in the absence of the priest, and
some old man was usually selected for the duty.
He employed as the form some rhapsody of his own,
with ceremonies to match. Thus he put salt into
the water. The child was wrapped in a she-
goat's skin. The parents were put outside the
door. The old man, holding the child, asked the
mother from what maladies she wished the child
to be preserved and what good fortune she
wished it to enjoy. Receiving answers he poured
water on the child, and said, I baptize you for
your father and mother, for your spouse and

80

children, for your relatives and friends, and I
warrant you and preserve you from such maladies
and misfortunes etc. In hearing [of] this abuse,
the priests discovered one who had received no
other baptism. He was thirty five years old and
was married and he had already approached the
sacraments.'

The words *are strictly observed in conscientiously*
are substituted for *better kept than those of
Blood* deleted.

Gossip relation, Gossip is substituted for *ghostly.*

This the Romans observe: the added comment is
probably that of the Rev John Beaton. In the Roman
Catholic Church spiritual relationship is an
impediment to marriage. It is interesting to find
this tradition surviving in the Highlands in the
late seventeenth century.

34. FOSTERING

Generally they send their children out to Foster
til 6.7.8. or 9 years of age.
They, to whom the children are sent, to be
fostered get a part such a portion of Goods freely
for the use of the Foster child and so doe the
Parents, which the Foster Father engageth to keep
for the Foster child *at the Parents expences*, and
return it with the product when he cometh to years.
He who giveth his child to be fostered, bestoweth on the Foster-mother a silver Broach which is
worn on the Breast or a Necklace of stones which
are of greatest Account amongst them.
The Foster Father lyimayet leavs a legacy to
the Foster child as well as to his own children.
He has a Barn's part of the Gear. Mr Beaton.

Editor's Notes

The closeness of the relationship established
by fosterage in the Highlands is proverbial. *'An
co'dhalta nach dearbh àite, 's mairg a dh'àraich
duine riamh'* 'The foster-child that proves it not,
pity him that reared' and *'Comhdhaltas gu ciad is
càirdeas gu fichead'* 'Fostership to a hundred,
blood-relationship to twenty degrees' (Nicolson,
Gaelic Proverbs 26) are sayings which illustrate
this. See also Section 21 here.
See the MS History of Craignish for 'a piece of
Hystory that for so much seems to attest how
sacredly the Highlanders esteem'd the Relation of
Coaltship,' which the writer himself (Alexander
Campbell, who wrote around 1720) 'have seen in
great vogue and experienc'd the good fruits thereof.' This relates how an old Highlander in the
fifteenth century lamented the death of his foster-
son more than the death of four of his own sons in
a fight with a band of robbers, and tried to kill

one of his own surviving sons for the cowardice
of which he accused him in allowing his 'coalt'
to be killed in the fight. (S.H.S. Miscellany IV
224-226).

a Barn's part of the Gear: i.e. a child's share of
the foster parent's moveable property, as a child
would under Scots law.

35. DREAMS

They greatly observe Dreams (& [illegible] great
skil in Dreams). Ordinarily before the Death of
any Friend, they have some intimation of it by
Dreams; as by falling the upper Teeth, or any part
of the House[,] rain running through, undermining
&[c.]

Editor's Notes

The sentence in brackets is an insertion,
probably of an omission; the first two words of it
are mingled in writing with the word above, and
very difficult to make out.

On dreams, see D.McPH. 195; J.G.C.(S) 268.

36. LAKEWAKES

The poorest are kept after death one night, and then they use disguises, musec of all kinds (except the Bagpipe) dancing all exercises of Agility. Every one who comes into the place where the corps is, prayeth over it.

In some places they had singing women who were called to Lac-wakes, *and to funerals* where they diverted the company. They called them from one parish to an other.

Editor's Notes

LAKEWAKES = Lykewake, the watch by the dead.

they use disguises: this seems improbable. Did Kirkwood confuse burials with Hallowe'en, when disguises were worn? or did Lhuyd make a slip and copy 'dances' as 'disguises'? The custom of dancing at lykewakes in the Highlands was well known, and was commented on by writers, e.g. in a letter written on 10th June 1760 about a visit to Mull and Iona, Bishop Pococke remarked that:

'They spend commonly three days at funerals, one before and one after, and often more, especially those who come from far; and this time is spent in eating and drinking very plentifully; and the widow and children danced with others round the Corps till very lately.' (*Tour*, p.88)

See also Burt, II 107; Pennant, I 113; R.O. II 428, and Séan Ó Suilleabháin, *Irish Wake Amusements* (Cork, 1967).

37. BURIAL

They generally desire to be buryed with their
Ancestors.

The women make a crying while the corps is
carried and when they have done, the Piper plays
after the corps with his great pipe. When they
come to the churchyard all the women (who always
go along to the Burial place) make a hideous
Lamentation together and then they have their
particular Mournfull Song for their other Friends
that lye there.

They bury Strangers in a corner of the churchyard and they bury with them a penny which they
call the penny of Friendship;† thinking thereby
to make Friends among the Dead†.

They have great Feastings at their Burials and
all kind[s] of Music.

The[y] Bury Pipers with the mouth downwards. *Q.*
where.

Editor's Notes

desire to be buryed with their Ancestors: cp.
D.McPh. 203.

make a hideous Lamentation: 'Hideous' is substituted for 'great' in the MS. This 'hideous' lamentation was the coronach, an institution much disapproved of by the Presbyterian clergy. In 1642
the Synod of Argyll reprobated the practice and
even went so far as to threaten to invoke the
civil authority to suppress it, in the following
minute:

> 'Because it is common custome in some of the
> remottest pairts within this province of ignor-
> ant poore women to howle their dead into the
> graves, which commonly is called the corronach,
> a thing unseemly to be used in any true Christ-

86

ian kirk, where there is preacheing and pro-
fession of the comfortable resurrrection of the
dead, Wherefor for the restraineing thereof it
is ordained that every minister both in preacheing and catechiseing endeavore to inform them
how unseemely to Christians, and offensive to
God, and scandalouse to others the lyke practice
and carriage must be, And moreover, for curbing
of those that will be refractory and will not
receive information, intimation to be made
publictly by every minister in his own paroach
that the same is forbidden and ordained to be
punished, and after that every one that shall be
fund guilty of the said corronach shall stand
on Sunday in the church, and if they continue or
shall be fund ofter than once, then it is ordained that some of them be jogged and made examples
to the rest, And if this prevaill not that they
represent it by ane act of session unto My Lord
Marquesse [of Argyll] who has promised to take
ordour with the same.' (A.S.M. I 61).

See also R.O. 430-1, Burt II 108, and notes to
Section 36 here.

thinking thereby: this sentence was deleted in the
MS, possibly on the advice of the Rev John Beaton.

38. LORDS SUPPER

They are not at the Lords Supper to give the
Bread, from hand to hand, but every one takes to
himself. *Q. whether the Presbyterians do this.*

Editor's Notes

The reference is presumably to the arrangement
whereby the communicants sat round a long table,
and passed the bread to each other in a basket or
on a pewter plate. Moreover as shortbread was
often used, this helped to prevent the scattering
of crumbs. Alternatively the words 'they are not
... to give the Bread from hand to hand' would
mean that with all seated round a small table, the
basket or plate was placed in the centre and
'everyone takes to himself'. I am obliged to the
Rev Dr Bulloch, minister of Stobo, for this information, transmitted by the Rev W.Grant Anderson.
Lhuyd's query may have been due to his knowledge
that the writer of the *Collection* was an Episcopalian.

39. OBSERVATIONS OF DAYS

On Tuseday they yoak their ploughs and begin their sowing and their sheiring on [W]edensday. *They'l not begin any work on the* [illegible] *day of the year i.e. 3 of May.* They begin nothing on Saturnday. The 3^d of May is the great Dismal day.

† They think the L^{ds} Day is consecrat to ane Angel called *Domhin*†. They think water drawen on that day hath more vertue then [*sic*] upon an other day.

They say no common Exercise is lawfull on Sunday yet they think they may hunt the Fox and kil it if they light on it though in time of Sermon. *Query.*

Editor's Notes

On the Observation of Days, see R.O. 448-9; J.G.C.(W) 294-301.

3^d of May: see GWSU under LATHA (*Latha chòrr na Bliadhna*).

They think the L^{ds} Day, this improbable assertion is deleted in the MS, very probably on the contradiction of the Rev John Beaton.

40. SWEARING

The men swear by the hand of their Cheif. Men and woman [*sic*] sweareth by the Tutelar Saint of the Countrey, some swear by the hand of their Gossip who holds up their children. They swear by their Fathers hand, which if another doe, it is the greatest provocation.

Editor's Notes

For swearing by the chief's and the father's hand, see Martin 120. See also the MS History of Craignish, S.H.S. Miscellany IV 203, where it is related that the Toshach Bain Mac Eachairn 'swore the common oath of the ancient Scots, by our Father and Grand Fathers hands'; this was in the twelfth century. In the same MS it is later related (p.232) how an enraged lady is said to have replied to a condescending offer of marriage 'with the usual asseveration, Carle, by your Father and Goodsire's hands, I scorn to live with you upon such mean conditions.' This incident took place around 1500.

See also Nicolson's *Gaelic Proverbs*, 298. The expression occurs in one of Alexander MacDonald's poems, see HS45 p.61.

Men and woman, 'Men and' were substituted for 'the' deleted.

41. PUBLIK WORSHIP

In prayer they usually repeat after the minister;
and generally both men and women kneel at their
at their [sic] entring the church. They have their
private prayers.

42. BENEDICTIONS

In their Benedictions they usually wish their Benefactors, children and nephews to many Generations. Riches and honesty, and of safety from Friends Fraud and their enemies Foarce.

When they appeal to God as judge of their Integrity they look up to the sun and say, o Founder of yonder eye see and Judge.

Lhuyd's Note (Folio 29)

When they go out at night to shut the Window, he without says *benedicite*; and they within say *benedicat nos Deus* [may God bless us] and prays tow or three sentences.

Editor's Notes

o *Founder of yonder eye*, see note to Section 45.

43. SACRED PLACES

They have wells dedicat to certain Saints to which
hik people resort as Straphyllan in Perthshire.
   The Gentry have their burial places in Churches
and tho they sel their lands, will not alienat
them. Half a mile about the Kirk was a place of
refuge formerly. *Six miles (any way) from Y Columb
kil was a Refuge.*

Editor's Notes

Hik, presumably the word in the MS which Lhuyd was
not sure of was 'sik'.

44. THE MOON

When first they see the moon new, they turn themselves about thrice, and take up Grasses &c cast
towards it, and bless God for it. *Mr B. has seen
men doe it.*

Lhuyd's Note (Folio 31)

At the sight of the new moon they cut a crosse
in the ground saying I have wounded you or bled
you Dear [illegible] (viz. the earth) before I am
wounded: after which they hope not to be wounded
during the course of that moon.

Editor's Notes

For moon lore, see J.Carmichael Watson's
article on *Carmina Gadelica* in Yorkshire Celtic
Studies, I 33-37. See also C.G. III 274-305, and
Martin, 174; R.O. II 449; J.G.C.(W) 304-7.

45. THE SUN

They call the sun the eye of God.
When they cross (?) a water that is deep they
take hold of a cow's tayle and commit themselves
to the stream.
On their travelling they always lye in their
plaids. *Formerly* some marryd onely for a year and
a day and gave the woman a consideration at part-
ing. They marry at the new moon. *Q.*

Editor's Notes

Most of this section has nothing to do with the
sun. The sentence about crossing a river could be
referred to Section 12, and that about trial
marriages to Section 33.

They call the sun the eye of God: cp. the invoc-
ation C.G. III 306 beginning *'Sùil Dhé mhóir'*.
'Eye of great God'.

Formerly some marryd, the word 'Formerly' is an
insertion. Regarding trial marriages of a year,
see Martin 114. Martin says that 'this unreason-
able Custom was long ago brought in disuse'. For
the Borders, see Pennant II 91-2. But see also
A.E.Anton 'Handfasting in Scotland', *Scottish
Historical Review* XXXVII 89. The idea that such a
custom existed may have arisen from the existence
formerly in Scotland of marriage *per verbo de
futuro*. Some of the couples charged with fornica-
tion e.g. in the Argyll Synod Minutes may in fact
have been Catholics so married and awaiting the
possible coming of a priest at a time when there
were very few priests on the Highland mission.

46. CROSTARITH [CROIS-TÀRAIDH]

In sudden danger, they cleav a staf, and put a stick off it, burning it a litle, in which they send [?] from hand to hand, and all convene at the place appointed. *They doe not burn it but in case of Life or burning of houses &c. When one finds it sticking in a door 'tis death not to carry it to the next Town.*

Editor's Notes

This was the Fiery Cross of the Highlanders, used to summon the clans for warfare. In 1675 (for example) an Act of Adjournal alleged that Lauchlan MacLean of Brolas in Mull 'did convocate together armed men with swords, hagbuts, pistolls, durks and other weapons invasive ... In the moneth of April last bypast, upon the twenty-twa day, or ane or other of the days of the said moneth, without any order of law, at Kenlochnakeall, upon the lands of Knockteirmartein, extending to the number of three or four hundreth men, which they did, by sending through the isle of Mull, Morverne, and other places fyre croces for convocating of the country people in arms...' (H.P. I 305). This was done to resist the threatened foreclosure by the Argyll Campbells of the debts they held on the estates of the MacLeans of Duart. The foreclosure eventually took place.

See also Burt, II 122-3; Pennant I 212.

Town = village, township.

47. RARITIES

The Pear of Cstown sayd to be keep 300 years
The Beef of Borthwick Castle..
The Watdish of Bily in the Mersh
The Beaf pot of Nunraw
The craw egg at Canglton
Hauthiendame caves
Roslin College and house
The oily well near Edenb.
The monument at Dumbar
Tentallan well
In a loge in knaedail
Hidem^t cives and ward stones.

Editor's Notes

None of these places are in the Highlands. On
the other hand, several are in Mid and East
Lothian, Kirkwood's native part of the country.
It is evident that Lhuyd found some difficulty
in reading the original manuscript in this Section.
This is borne out by his own corrections, and the
fact that some of the words are unintelligible.
Lhuyd was also obviously writing hurriedly to
finish copying Kirkwood's manuscript.

Pear was first written *paer*. *Cstown* is written
over *Castoune* which is underlined. Perhaps Castle-
toun? There are several places of this name in
Scotland, of which the best known one is in Rox-
burghshire. *sayd* was first written *land*, then
altered to make sense, a sign of mechanical copying.

Beef of Borthwick Castle might be a mistake for
beel = shelter, or for *peel*, a tower.

Watdish is unintelligible; Lhuyd was clearly uncertain of the word. Bily is in the parish of

97

Preston and Bonkell in Berwickshire, also called the Merse.

Beaf pot = a pickling tub. The hollow out of which the River Annan rises is called the 'Deil's Beef-Tub' or the 'Marquis of Annandale's Beef-stand' (Pococke, *Tour* p.40). Perhaps something of the same kind is meant here.

craw = crow. *Canglton* (Congaltoun) is in Dirleton parish in East Lothian.

Hauthiendame is an obvious copying mistake for *Hawthornden*. *Caves* was first copied as *cates*, then corrected.

The last two lines are unintelligible to me. *Ward stones* suggests the Wardens' Dykes in the parish of Graitney and Reidkirk in Annandale, see Mac-Farlane's *Geographical Collections* I 385.

Borthwick, Hawthornden, Roslin house and chapel (not college) and the oily well at Liberton near Edinburgh, are all described in an undated, probably seventeenth century, account of Midlothian, author not named, in the same work, II 122-3:

'The Castle of Borthwick is a great and strong Tower all of Aslure work within and without, and of great height. the Wall thereof being about 15 feet of thickness. It has an excellent Wellspring in the bottom without digging, and a house of good lodgings and well lighted...

'Rosline standing upon Northesk is pleasantly situate upon the head of a Rock, having the Water running close by the foot of the Craig, and environed upon all sides with Woods. The entry thereof is at the top of the house by a Draw Bridge to the bridge upon the Water running by the foot thereof. The Vaults and houses thereof are cutted out of the whole Craig, and the stairs and passages descending thereto in like manner are cutted out of the whole Craig; so

that each Vault or house cutted out of the
whole Craig, consists of but one stone.
   'The Chappel of Rosline is the most curious
stone work in this kingdom, so that to the eye
of man, nothing can be more exquisitly wrought
upon stone.
   'Upon the east of Rosline at Hawthornden
there is a large Cove [= cave] with two or three
Rooms ilk one within another, having but one
entry, quilk is unpassable except at one part
where the entry goes along by the breadth of a
deal, having the Water 30 or 40 fathoms beneath
the face of the Craig, whereinto the said Cove
enters just above.
   'To the south of Libertoun Kirk there is a
Wellspring which sends up with the Water an Oyl
or rather a Balsam reasonable thick and fat.
This Balsam is gathered and preserved by the
Heritors 10 months of the Year, and is a
soveraign cure for wrests, Akings &c.'

   These features are also described in a Latin
account of Midlothian in the second volume of the
Geographical Collections, pp.620-1 and in translation, 634-5.
   Tantallon Castle, 'situate on a Rock ten
fathoms above the sea' is described in an account
of East Lothian, (no name, no date) in the third
volume of the work cited, p.113, but nothing is
said about its well.

The monument at Dumbar: Dunbar was Kirkwood's
birthplace. The monument is graphically described
by Bishop Pococke in a letter dated 23rd September
1760:

   'At the east end [of the church at Dunbar] is
a magnificent monument covering the three windows,
with this inscription on it. Here lyeth the body
of the reight hon[le] George Earl of Dvnbar Baron
Howme of Barwick, Lord heigh Tressr. of Scotland,

99

Knight of the most noble order of the Garter,
And one of his Mat^te most noble privie Covnsell
whoe depted this life the xxix day of Jannvary
MDCXI.

'He is represented in the mantle of the order
as Kneeling (at a Desk with a book on it) on a
Cushion placed on a Sarcophagus, on each side of
him are Cariatides of men in Coats of Mail, holding with one hand the Arms on a shield; They
support an Entablature upon which on each side
are the Statues of Justice & Charity with a
Corinthian pilaster on each of them, between
them is the inscription, and above on the Entablature on each side is a Coast of Arms, between these is a Sarcophagus and on the middle
of it seems to have been a Coast of Arms; The
Execution and Design is very fine and it is said
to be Italian, on it is this Motto, Homo ditat,
Deus beat.' (*Tour*, p.321).

APPENDIX

NOTES ON *EDWARD LHUYD IN THE SCOTTISH HIGHLANDS*

1. Lhuyd's meeting with the Rev John Beaton

There is a reference to this in an unpublished
letter from Lhuyd to Sir Robert Sibbald, written
at Londonderry on 20th April, 1700, of which a
copy is preserved in one of Sibbald's notebooks.
I am grateful to Mr I.C.Cunningham for drawing my
attention to this.

'I had the good fortune to meet with an
ancient Irish Vocabulary written on parchment
severall centuries since, but tis only of the
Words that were at that time obsolete, explained
by the Words then in use; but even these are now
so far Antiquated, that the critics I have
hitherto mett with could make little of them.
Mr John Beatoun, to whom I showed it, said that
[it] alone was worth all my tyme and expence in
these two Kingdomes, *sed qui amant, ipsi sibi
somnia fingunt.*
'This Mr Beatoun showed me three very Large
Leavs on parchment, of the Work of one Carbri
Lefarhair in Irish. This Carbri he sayd was a
Heathen and Leaved [*sic*] about the year 200,
which if true, I look upon this Fragment, as a valu-
able Curiosity, as being the oldest writing in
our British Isles we have heard of as extant in
our tyme, and perhaps containing some light as
to the doctrine of the old Druids. And if he
performs his promise, I am to receive his Copy
of it this evening, which I shall bring to
Flaherty the author of the Ogygia to be inter-
preted, for Mr Beatoun owns he can make nothing
of it.'

The *ancient Irish Vocabulary* could be MS H.2.

15b. of Trinity College, Dublin, which is known to
have been in Lhuyd's collection, and which contains several glossaries.

For the *Carbri Lefarhair* MS, see ELSH pp.12-14
and 44-51. In Gaelic tradition Cairbre Lifeachair
is said to have been killed at the battle of
Gabhra in A.D. 284; the MS in question has been
identified as the second part of MS I of the
National Library of Scotland, described by
Professor MacKinnon as probably dating back to
the fourteenth century.

2. *More on the Rev John Beaton*

The Rev John Beaton, Episcopalian minister of
Kilninian in Mull, last learned member of the
great Beaton medical family, and Edward Lhuyd's
most important Scottish Highland informant, whose
comments are frequently added by Lhuyd to the copy
he made of Kirkwood's *Collection*, is the author of
a twelve-verse Gaelic poem 'Upon the Revolution
and Silencing the Episcopall Ministers in Mull &c'
that is preserved in the Hector MacLean MS in the
Public Archives of Nova Scotia, and which was
printed, with some rather startling emendations,
by the Rev A.MacLean Sinclair in *The Gaelic Bards
from 1411 to 1715* (Charlottetown, 1890), pp.144-
147.

The poem describes very eloquently the bewilder-
ment and sufferings of the inhabitants of the
island of Mull under the Argyll takeover following
their foreclosure on the estates of the MacLeans
of Duart. Beaton's own sufferings as a 'poor
sojourning Clergyman' following the abolition of
Episcopacy and the ousting of the Episcopal clergy
from their parishes are described in the following
verse:

> *'S anabarr ri ràitinn,*
> *Ged bu Phàganaich 'nan aidmheil iad-*

Fear theagaisg an slànaidh dhaibh,
  'S 'gan toirt o chàs an t-seacharain,
Gun chiont, gun àdhbhar
  Ach air ràdh nam factoran
An déidh seirbheis na Sàbaide
  Gun fhios cia 'n t-àit' an caidil e.

'It is extraordinary to relate - even if they
were pagans in their religion - the man who is
teaching salvation to them, and bringing them
from the danger of error, without blame or cause,
but on the order of the factors, after the
Sabbath service knows not where he will sleep.'

It may be noticed here that in the fourth line
of the second verse the editor has substituted the
word *dream* for *nation* (*nàisean*) of the original MS
text, to the disadvantage of the rhyme; and that
in the fifth verse the fifth line, which reads
Nach faic thu na socainn in the printed version,
with *socan* glossed 'fieldfare', the MS reads *Nach
faic thu na sho'cean*, which must stand for
seobhcan, 'hawks', a familiar expression in such
poems, whereas the word *socan* 'fieldfare' is
hardly known in Scottish Gaelic, and in any case
would not rhyme with *bòidheach* in the next line.
  There are some interesting remarks about the
Beaton manuscripts in Robert Armstrong's Gaelic
Dictionary (which, incidentally, is the only Scottish source for *socan* = fieldfare) under the head-
ing OLLAMH:

'A succession of an order of literati named
ollamh existed in Mull from time immemorial,
until after the middle of the last century [the
Dictionary was published in 1825]. Their writ-
ings were all in Gaelic, to the amount of a
large chestful. Dr Smith says that the remains
of their treasure were brought as a literary
curiosity to the library of the Duke of Chandos,
and perished in the wreck of that nobleman's

fortune. The last of the order was the famous old Doctor John Breton' [*sic*: the Doctor John Beaton who died on 19th November 1657].

3. *Ferron Garyv thîr* (ELSH p.73)

In his interesting article 'A Lost MacMhuirich Manuscript' (*Scottish Gaelic Studies*, X 158) Dr Alan Bruford has shown, with evidence from the papers of J.F.Campbell of Islay, that these words should be transliterated *Fear o'n Gharbh-thìr*, 'The Man from the Rough Land', and that this was the title of a large MS collection of Early Modern Irish heroic and romantic tales, taken away from South Uist by MacNeil of Barra, and unfortunately lost. The words have nothing to do with any game preserve of Clanranald.

4. *Rev John MacLean* (ELSH p.23)

Apart from his poem in praise of Lhuyd, printed in the Introduction to *Archaeologia Britannica*, several pieces by the Rev John MacLean, who succeeded John Beaton as minister of Kilninian in 1702, have been preserved. One of these, *Craobh ar sinnsir, cha chrion o thainig*, a lament for the chief of the Clan MacLean, presumably Sir John MacLean, of Duart, who died in 1716. This is printed in the Inverness Collection of Gaelic poetry, 1821, p.183. Three others of his poems, a love poem, an elegy, and a lament for the decline of the Clan MacLean, are printed in A.MacLean Sinclair's *The Gaelic Bards from 1715 to 1765* (Charlottetown, 1892), pp.54-68. His poetry reveals clear Jacobite sympathies. He was an interesting, and sympathetic man and it is to be regretted that his personal papers were not preserved.

104

5. *The MacLean of Duart debt* (ELSH p.18)

The MacLeans of Duart were financially embarrassed long before 1651. This is clear from the fact that in 1622 Sir Rory MacKenzie of Coigeach stated in an action against Sir John MacDougall of Dunolly that his (Sir Rory's) brother-in-law Hector Mac-Lean of Duart was being pursued both for arrears of official taxes as well as for personal debts 'quhairby his house was lyke to be ruined' and that 'Sir Rorie out of regaird to him and [the] standing of his house' had 'not only tane on him the burden of the said Hector's debts but the yeirly payment of his Majesties dutie extending to tua thousand fyve hundred merkis, for which he had got a rycht to the said Hector's estate[1]'.

Hector MacLean's heir, Hector younger of Duart, married Margaret, daughter of Sir Rory MacLeod of Dunvegan, in 1623, and as the editor of the *Book of Dunvegan* remarked[2], 'McLane seems to have been in very low water financially, as he is able to settle any lands in life rent on his future wife only with the consent of Sir Rorie MacKenzie of Cogeach, into whose hands it is stated the lands to be settled had passed, viz. the fifty-three merk 10s. land of Morovane and the thirty-merk land of Aros in Mull, which, however, Sir Rorie has allowed to be settled on the payment of 10,000 merks, the whole business to be settled on such terms "as sal be thocht expedient by the men of law."'

Four years later Hector MacLean of Duart granted a bond for 5360 merks at 10% to the tutors of Charles, son of Sir Rorie MacKenzie of Coigeach[3]. Between then and the end of 1635 Lauchlan MacLean

1. *Collectanea de Rebus Albanicis* (1847). p.154.
2. *Book of Dunvegan* I 55.
3. *ibidem* 178.

of Duart, Hector's successor, borrowed 25,000 more merks (a merk was two-thirds of a £) from a certain John Fairholme: this debt was discharged by John MacLeod of Dunvegan, to whom and to whose heirs the claim against the MacLeans of Duart was transferred[3]. From Lauchlan Mor MacLean of Duart, who died in 1598 after a lifetime of aggression against the MacDonalds of Islay, the MacLeans of Duart appear to have been wildly extravagant. The full story of their debts and final ruin has yet to be written. Their transactions, which show how easy it was for early seventeenth century Highland chiefs to raise money on the security of their estates, totally disprove the popular myth that clan lands were owned in common by the clan before 1746.

6. *Symphoniaci* (ELSH p.34)

The Gaelic equivalent is probably *lucht seanma*.

7. *Hastening Death* (ELSH p.52)

'In Morayshire, at present, if a dying person struggles hard and long, and seems to have difficulty, and to suffer much, in departing, it is quite common to unlock all the doors etc. etc. in the house, as if by some magic spell the departing spirit of the sufferer were confined, they know not where, or how, by some lock or knot, near his person. I have known it done, but could never procure any other account of the ceremony, than they did it *because folks used* to do it.' (Robert Jameson *Popular Ballads and Songs*, II 184).

3. *ibidem* 178.

8. *Cakes given to owners of horses* (FLSH p.59)

Cp. Duncan Fraser, *Highland Perthshire*, (Montrose, 1969) pp.39-40, for an account similar to that of Pennant.

9. *The Roedeer and the Hare* (ELSH p.62)

Ycheldir is the word used by Lhuyd for the High-lands, and I think it is more likely that the sentence here means 'if they encounter hares in the Highlands, it is sign of misfortune'. It is well known that witches were supposed in the High-lands to take the form of hares, cp. J.G.C.(W) 33.

In a letter written on 10th June 1760 at Lis-more, after his visit to Mull and Iona, Bishop Pococke remarked that 'They have neither hares, partriges, nor the Roe Deer; but plenty of red Deer, the black game and grouse' on Mull, (Scot-tish History Society, first series I 89).

10. *The Badger* (ELSH p.64)

The late T.C.Lethbridge wrote me, apropos of this passage, that in Devonshire it is said that it is possible to tell the age of a badger by lifting it up by the tail and counting the rings round its anus. Possibly this is the idea Lhuyd was trying to express.

11. *The Golden Eagle* (ELSH p.65)

Bishop Pococke, op. cit. p.125, wrote from Tongue in Sutherland on 1st July 1760 that 'the eagles will, they say, kill a hart by seizing them about the neck and fluttering their wings in their eyes.' In a footnote, the editor of the volume refers to 'an account of a desperate struggle between an eagle and a stag' described in the *Scotsman* of 11th December 1884.

? mel. here cannot, in view of the instances occurring where Lhuyd inserted it in his copy of Kirkwood's *Collection*, refer to lightning.

12. *The Raven* (p.66) *and The Magpie* (p.67)

See Section 8 of Kirkwood's *Collection* here.

BIBLIOGRAPHY

ALLEN, J.Romilly. *The Early Christian Monuments of Scotland*. Edinburgh, 1903.

ANTON, A.E. *'Handfasting' in Scotland*. Scottish Historical Review, vol. XXXVII, 1958.

ANDERSON, A.O. *Early Sources of Scottish History, A.D. 500-1286*. Edinburgh, 1922. (A.O.A.)

BIRCH, Thomas, M.A. and F.R.S., *The Life of the Honourable Robert Boyle*. London, 1744.

BOSWELL, James. *Journal of a Tour to the Hebrides with Samuel Johnson*, 1773. Ed. Frederick A. Pottle, New York, 1962.

BRUFORD, Alan. *A Lost MacMhuirich Manuscript*. Scottish Gaelic Studies, vol. X, 1965.

BURT, Captain Edward. *Letters from a Gentleman in the North of Scotland to His Friend in London*. (Written c.1730). Fifth edition, 2 vols., London 1822.

CAMERON GILLIES, H. *Regimen Sanitatis*. Glasgow, 1911.

CAMPBELL, Alexander. *The Manuscript History of Craignish*. Ed. Herbert Campbell. Scottish History Society Miscellany IV. 1926. (A full MS version of this is in the family papers of the editor of the present book).

CAMPBELL, J.Gregorson. *Superstitions of the Scottish Highlands, collected entirely from Oral Sources*. Glasgow, 1900. (J.G.C.(S).)

CAMPBELL, J.Gregorson. *Witchcraft and Second Sight in the Highlands and Islands of Scotland. Tales and Traditions collected entirely from Oral Sources*. Glasgow, 1902. (J.G.C.(W).)

CAMPBELL, John L. *Highland Songs of the Forty-Five*. Edinburgh, 1933. (HS45)

CAMPBELL, John L. *Stories from South Uist*. London, 1961.

CAMPBELL, John L., and COLLINSON, F. *Hebridean Folksongs*. Oxford, 1969. (HF).

CAMPBELL, John L. *The Tour of Edward Lhuyd in Ire-

land in 1699 and 1700. Celtica, vol.V 218-228.
(TELI).

CAMPBELL, John L., and THOMSON, Derick. *Edward Lhuyd in the Scottish Highlands, 1699-1700.* Oxford, 1963. (ELSH).

CAMPBELL, John L., and HALL, Trevor H. *Strange Things. The Enquiry by the Society for Psychical Research into Second Sight in the Scottish Highlands...and the stories and folklore collected by Fr Allan McDonald of Eriskay.* London, 1968. (S.T.)

CARMICHAEL, Alexander. *Carmina Gadelica. Hymns and Incantations, with Illustrative Notes on Words, Rites, and Customs, Dying and Obsolete: Orally Collected in the Highlands and Islands of Scotland and Translated into English.* Six volumes, Edinburgh 1928-1971. (C.G.)

CARSWELL, Bishop John. *Foirm nan Nurrnuidheadh agas freasdal na Sacramuinteadh* (translation of John Knox's Liturgy, printed in 1567). Ed. Thomas MacLauchlan LL.D., Edinburgh, 1873

CLARKE, E.D. *A Tour in Scotland in the summer and autumn of 1797.* (Printed in vol.I pp.277-429 of *The Life and Remains of Edward Daniel Clarke,* by the Rev William Otter, London, 1825.)

FRASER, Rev James. *Chronicles of the Frasers. The Wardlaw Manuscript.* Edited by William MacKay. Scottish History Society vol.47, first series. Edinburgh, 1905.

GUNTHER, R.T. *Life and Letters of Edward Lhuyd.* Early Science in Oxford, vol.xiv. Oxford, 1945.

HUME BROWN, P. *Scotland before 1700.* Edinburgh, 1893.

KEMP, Daniel William. *Tours in Scotland, 1747, 1750, 1760. By Richard Pococke, Bishop of Meath.* Scottish History Society, First Series, vol.I Edinburgh, 1887.

KIRK, Robert. *The Secret Commonwealth of Elves, Fauns, and Fairies.* Edited by Andrew Lang. Stirling, 1933. (Kirk).

110

MACCULLOCH, John. *The Highlands and Western Isles of Scotland*. Four volumes. London, 1824.

McDONALD, Rev Fr Allan. *Gaelic Words and Expressions from South Uist and Eriskay*. Dublin, 1958 (GWSU).

McDONALD, Rev Fr Allan. Manuscript folklore collection; made in South Uist and Eriskay between 1887 and 1905. Similar to that made in Tiree by the Rev J.Gregorson Campbell.

MACFARLANE, Walter. *Geographical Collections relating to Scotland*. Edited by Sir Arthur Mitchell, K.C.B. Scottish History Society, first series vols.51-53.

MACKENZIE, William (secretary of the original Crofters' Commission), *Gaelic Incantations and Charms of the Hebrides*. Transactions of the Gaelic Society of Inverness, XVIII 97-182 (1892).

MACKINNON, Professor Donald. *A Descriptive Catalogue of Gaelic Manuscripts in the Advocates' Library Edinburgh, and Elsewhere in Scotland*. Edinburgh, 1912. (G.MSS.S).

MACLEAN, Rev Donald, D.D. *Highland Libraries in the Eighteenth Century*. Transactions of the Gaelic Society of Inverness, vol.XXXI 69-97 (T.G.S.I.) Inverness, 1927.

MACLEAN, Rev Donald, D.D. *Life of the Rev Robert Kirk*. Transactions of the Gaelic Society of Inverness, vol.XXXI 328-366.

MACLEAN SINCLAIR, A. *Gaelic Bards from 1411 to 1715*. Charlottetown, 1890.

MACPHALL, Sheriff J.R.N. *Highland Papers*. Scottish History Society, second series vols.5, 12, 20; third series vol.IV.

MACPHERSON, Donald. *Melodies from the Gaelic, and Original Poems, with Notes on the superstitions of the Highlanders*. London, 1824. (D.McPh.).

MACTAVISH, Duncan C. *Minutes of the Synod of Argyll*. (ed.) Scottish History Society, third series vols.XXXVII and XXXVIII. (A.S.M.).

MARTIN, Martin. *A Description of the Western*

Islands of Scotland...The Second Edition, very much Corrected. London, 1716. (Martin).

MARTIN, Martin. *A Late Voyage to St Kilda*. London, 1698. (Martin St Kilda).

NECKER DE SAUSSURE, *Voyage en Écosse et aux Îles Hébrides*. Three volumes. Geneva, 1821.

NICOLSON, Sheriff Alexander. *A Collection of Gaelic Proverbs and Familiar Phrases*. Edinburgh, 1881.

Ó SUILLEABHÁIN, Sean, *Irish Wake Amusements*. Cork, 1967.

PENNANT, Thomas. *A Tour in Scotland; MDCCLXIX*. Two volumes. Fifth edition. London, 1790.

ROSSI, Dr Mario. *Text-Criticism of Robert Kirk's Secret Commonwealth*. Edinburgh Bibliographical Society Transactions, vol.III 255-268, sessions 1954-55. (Translated by M.I.Johnston).

ROSSI, Dr Mario. *Il Cappellano delle Fate. Con testo originale e traduzione del Regno Segreto di Robert Kirk*. Storia e Pensiero, Naples, 1964. (the MS La III 551 text of the *Secret Commonwealth*, with introductory material, Italian translation, notes and apparatus: ICDF).

SHARP, L.W. *Early Letters of Robert Wodrow*. Scottish History Society, third series vol.XXIV. 1937.

SHAW, Margaret Fay. *Folksongs and Folklore of South Uist*. London, 1955. (FFSU).

SINCLAIR, Sir John, Bart. *The Statistical Account of Scotland. Drawn up from the Communications of the Ministers of the Different Parishes*. Twenty-one volumes. Edinburgh, 1791-99. (Usually referred to as the 'Old Statistical Account'). (O.S.A.).

SKENE, W.F. *The Highlanders of Scotland*. Edited with Excursus and Notes by Alexander MacBain. Stirling, 1902.

SPALDING CLUB. *The Sculptured Stones of Scotland*. Two volumes: Aberdeen, 1856; Edinburgh, 1867.

TOLMIE, Frances. *One Hundred and Five Songs of Occupation from the Western Isles of Scotland*.

Journal of the Folk Song Society. London, 1911.

WATSON, J.Carmichael. *Carmina Gadelica*. Yorkshire Celtic Studies I 33-56. (Transactions for 1937-38).

WATSON, W.J. *Cliar Sheanchain*. Celtic Review, IV 80-88. Edinburgh, 1907-8.

WATSON, W.J. *Scottish Verse from the Book of the Dean of Lismore*. Scottish Gaelic Texts Society. Edinburgh, 1937.

GLOSSARIAL INDEX

References are to the numbers of the Sections; numbered followed by L refer to Lhuyd's notes that follow some of the Sections.

A Scottish Gaelic

Amhran, òran, 15L
amm sgobadh nam
  Faoilleach, 1L

Bealltainn bheag, 1L
Bealltainn mhór, 1L
brianan, 26
brochan, 7

Calluinn, Colluinn, 1L
cam-rann, 20
caorthainn, 27
Ceart-chomach, 7
Céitein, 1L
Céitein earraich, 1L
Céitein samhraidh, 1L
ceòth[r?]om ?, 1L
Ciadain an luaithrigh,
  1L
Clann Ó Duibhne, 6
Cliar Sheanchain, 20
Cóicthigheas Gearrain,
  1L
Cói' la deug na Dàmhair,
  1L
colpa, 21
coinnmheadh, 13
comhdhalta, 21
crois folachd, 11
crois-tàraidh, 46
crònan, 15L
cuid oidhche, 7, 17

damh ursainn, 21
dàn dìreach, 20
deoch an doruis, 16
Diardaoin Màrtain, 1L
Diblin, 1
diot là, 7
Domhan, 39
Dòmhnach Càsg, 1L
Dòmhnach nan Slat, 1L

each colpa, 21
eachlach ùrlair, 7

Faoilleach, Faoilteach, 1
Faoilleach earraich, 1L
Faoilleach geamhraidh, 1L
Feadag, 1
Féill Cholum Cille, 1L
Féill na Croiche, 1L
Féill Seirbh, 1
Féill Sheathain, 1
fisiche, 8

gall-òglach, 10
gaoth ro'n leabhar, 27
Gearran borb, 1L
Gearrshìon, 1

iorram, 15L
Iuchar, 1

Là Bealltainn, 1L
lòn-chraois, 7
luinneag, 15L

Lùnasdal, 1L

Màrt-inid, 1L
mìos an Fhaoillich, 1L
mìos marbh, 1L

obaidh air shùil, 27
ollamh, 28

Seachdain nan Ceithir là
  Feadaig, 1L
sgaball, 10

tàbhairne, 25
tapadh *gle gioch* ?, 27L
teampull Chliamain, 26L

B *Scots Words*

airth, 8
areage, 17

bair, 2, bear, 12
barn, 34
beaf pot, 47
bennadistie, 2
bitles, 25
boals, 8
board, 7
boat = barrel, 27
bread, 2
budget, 30
bullet = boulder, 14

coag, 12
come speed, 24
corby, 8
craag, 2
craw, 47
criel, 19
croik, 8
cummers, comers, 33

diet, 7

fat = vat, 7
fey, 24
folding, 19
foyson, faison, 7

gear, 34
goodwill, 17, 32
gossips, 33
gowgow, 8

haggas, 7
hallinshakers, 7
hareshaw, 33
head and throwes, 5
healf, ? 18

jockies, 9

kinred, 11

lakewakes, 36
leen = eleven, 2
lyimayet ??? 34

marled, 5
meer, 18, 33
melt, 22
moneth, 1
mortclaith, 3

plyes, 25
propines, 5
pyots, 8

quairrs ??? 5

ran = rowan, 27

rock, 33
ruffies, 22

sap, 33
seen = seven, 2
servets, 7
sheers, 8
sheilds = sheals, 4
speed vb. 26
spraing, 5

stenting, 17
sungate, 25

? toilman, 7 (MS *tall-man*)
torn, 23
Tramontan, 28

watdish ??? 47
weason, 22
weik, 22